TITCHFIELD
AN ANCIENT PARISH

ISBN: 978 0 9508131 6 5

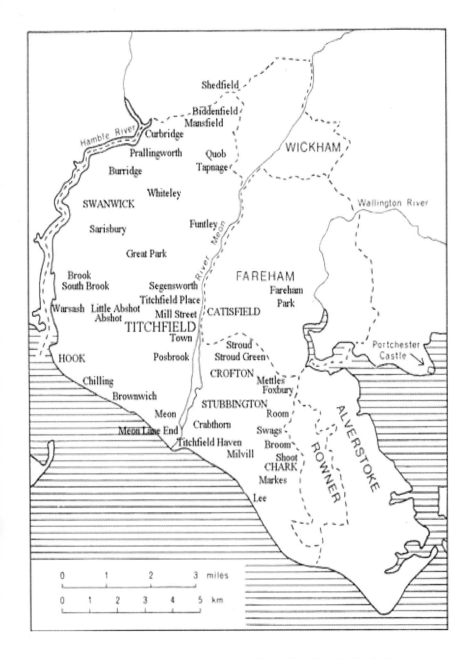

The Ancient Parish of Titchfield
Identifiable Locations in the Parish Register 1589-1634

TITCHFIELD

AN ANCIENT PARISH

Edited for the Titchfield History Society by George Watts

Editorial Committee: Ken Groves, Keith Hayward, Paul Hawkins, Annie Mitchell, John Mitchell, George Watts.

Dedicated to Dr. Kenneth Dunton
[1930-2010]

Titchfield History Society 2011

450 SAXON TICEFELDA 1066

FOREWORD

This is the third in a series of books on the history of Titchfield village and parish written for the Titchfield History Society. It follows Titchfield: A History, published in 1982, and Titchfield: A Place in History, published in 1989. The title of the present volume Titchfield: An Ancient Parish, has been chosen because for 1300 years Titchfield, with its parish church of St. Peter's, was not only the largest parish in Hampshire, but also the centre of a great estate which stretched from Warsash and Swanwick on the west, Crofton, Stubbington and Lee-on-the-Solent on the east, and north to Curbridge and Funtley. The volume therefore contains articles both on the village itself and on many parts of that wider parish.

Although it is arranged in a rough chronological order, this volume is not intended to be a continuous narrative. It is a collection of articles, both short and long, about many of the people, places, issues and problems which have featured during those 1300 years. It is a new collection: many very interesting topics - for instance the early Saxon foundation of St. Peter's, and Henry Cort's pioneering iron-process - dealt with in the earlier volumes, are not repeated here. Some topics have been reconsidered in the light of evidence accumulating in the years since 1989: they include the early 17th century estate map, and the 'shutting out' of the Meon estuary in 1611. But we now also know that there was an Iron Age site at Fernhill Farm, that the village of Hook had its own medieval chapel, that Arthur Lisle, the last Plantagenet, lived at Segensworth, and Henry Timberlake, 'the great Traviller', at Chilling - and much more. Cover picture is Patsy Popely leading Titchfield Carnival.

Each of the three volumes has been put together by an editorial committee made up of members of the Titchfield History Society. In 2011 it consisted of Ken Groves, Paul Hawkins, Keith Hayward, Annie Mitchell, John Mitchell and George Watts. We hope that you will enjoy this new book.

> Shown on the opposite page is the first frame of the Titchfield Tapestries, a series of seven drawings designed by artist John Harper. It depicts the village history and was produced by Tessa Short and a team of needle workers using stump work. The set of seven frames may usually be seen in the Titchfield Parish Room.

CONTENTS

Foreword   5

The Titchfield area during the Stone Age   8

Late Iron Age/Romano British site at Upper Segensworth   13

Crofton Old Church   15

Titchfield Abbey; its foundation and abbots   22

A chapel for Hook; a mediaeval dispute   27

Richard II and the fish pond   36

Dating Titchfield's buildings   39

The Titchfield Beacon   46

Margaret of Anjou   48

The Last Plantagenet   49

Bee boles at Place House   52

Chilling and the Dudley conspiracy   55

An early 17th century map of Titchfield and surrounding area   59

The Meon estuary   67

The Titchfield Canal or New River   68

The "old" sluice at Hill Head harbour   78

The sea lock   84

Titchfield Canal   86

The closure of Titchfield Haven   88

Mary Browne, second Countess of Southampton   99

Elizabeth Vernon, third Countess of Southampton   101

Henry Timberlake   103

Charles II and Queen Henrietta Maria in Titchfield   107

Titchfield Square   111

One Thomas or two?   112

A tragic romance   116

The Coach & Horses public house   117

Titchfield Haven water meadows   121

The Ives family   127

Admiral John Bourmaster   130

The Hornby family of Bombay and Hook   137

Sir Henry Warden Stanley Chilcott   141

Sarisbury Court   146

Titchfield's first bypass   150

Sarisbury Green in wartime   155

The Hurdens; three sons of Titchfield   157

The beer houses and inns   160

Titchfield Doctors   169

Nurse Gardner   174

Lee-on-the-Solent and its associations   175

Lee School   181

Holly Hill Woodland Park   182

Titchfield Haven National Nature Reserve   185

Premonstratensian Canons in Titchfield, 2011   186

1300 years of Titchfield History   189

Postscript, further reading and index.   193

THE TITCHFIELD AREA DURING THE STONE AGE PERIOD.

In Britain the period which we refer to as the Stone-age is currently recognised as covering a temporal span of c.750,000 years. To allow sections of this long period to be individually studied it has been broken down into three main groups, the earliest, which is known as the 'Palaeolithic' (or Old Stone-age), is followed by the 'Mesolithic' (or Middle Stone-age), and then by the 'Neolithic' (or New Stone-age); each of these three main groups are once again broken down into sub-sections, which may for example be termed earlier (lower) or later (upper) parts of each of the three main groups. Within local boundaries there occurs at Rainbow Bar, Hill Head, a lower Palaeolithic site which has, since its discovery by the late Chris Draper almost 60 years ago, (1) been shown to produce artefacts that are recognised as being of 'Clactonian' type, and are given that name because of their similarity to those artefacts which were recovered at the type site at Clacton-on- Sea, Essex.

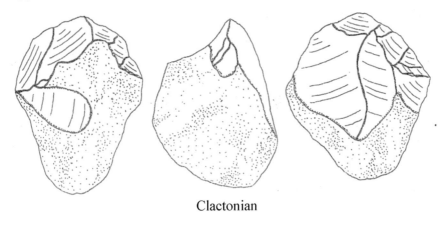

Clactonian

Rainbow Bar is an enigmatic site and remains a geological problem. It sits below the surface of the Solent for most of each 24 hour period making any possibly helpful excavation investigation very difficult to undertake. Perhaps the most puzzling aspect presented by the site is why or how this concentration of Clactonian artefacts appear on or close to the surface over such a small area. Artefacts of Clactonian type are not found in the locally occurring low-level gravel cliffs, or at other shoreline gravel exposures in the area. Many thousand stone artefacts have been recovered which have been crudely formed using as the raw material the pebbles and cobbles which make up the body of Rainbow Bar.(2). Details of these recoveries have been published and the items have been donated to Museums and Academic Establishments.

The Hack Collection, Dept. of Archaeology, University of Southampton,.for instance. Several M.A. theses have been submitted using the local collections from Rainbow Bar as their basis. Geologists have shown that Britain's land surfaces and sea - levels have been subjected to immense and often repeated changes throughout the Holocene and the preceding Pleistocene periods. It is accepted that Britain was once part of mainland Europe. During the last few decades

Brian Hack and colleagues at Rainbow Bar

discoveries have been made at sites which suggest that Early Man was present in Europe as long as a million years ago. It is in Man's nature to explore, and when conditions make it necessary, to migrate. After 13 years of studying and collecting at Rainbow Bar the writer is no closer to knowing who made these artefacts or when he made them, or what was his intention. Back in 1996 a very wise Archaeologist told the writer that in his opinion both Archaeological and Geological experts will meet their 'Waterloo' at Rainbow Bar. I now suspect that he may have been correct.

Stone artefacts which are attributable to a later period than the 'Clactonian' but still within the Palaeolithic period have been recovered from the local shoreline and from within the gradually eroding locally occurring low-level gravel cliffs. These artefacts are known as hand axes and are referred to as being of 'Acheulian' type after the type site at St Acheul in France where they were first recognised. These flint hand axes invariably display a far greater degree of craftsmanship in their manufacture than those presented by 'Clactonian' work, which is often shown to be the result of just a few flake removals from a broken or deliberately split flint pebble or cobble in the production of a working edge. The makers of both the Clactonian and the Acheulean type artefacts were hunter-gatherers, and these people are attributable to a lower or earlier part of the Palaeolithic period.

Evidence has been found locally for the presence of the last of our hunter-gather ancestors. These were the Mesolithic (or Middle Stone-age) people. They produced stone tools such as flint axes and picks, but are more readily recognised by their small flint tools known as microliths. These small flint flakes were often set end to end in a wooden or bone handle to make composite projectile points or cutting implements. Examples of both Mesolithic type axes and microliths have been recovered, albeit in small numbers, from Rainbow Bar.

Earth removal during gravel pit extraction between Meon Hamlet and the River suggest the presence of 'Neolithic' (or New Stone-age) people. A Jade Axe head and flint sickle. Apparently item i/ is held at Winchester Museum. A cast of item ii/ was displayed in a frame on a wall in Titchfield

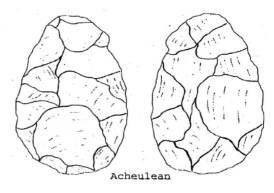

Acheulean

Church, the whereabouts of the original is not known to the writer. Flint scrapers and arrowheads which are typologically attributable to the Neolithic stone-age can sometimes be found as widespread scatters over our area. Our Neolithic ancestors were the first farmers and animal raisers to appear in Britain. No definitive settlement site of this period is known in the immediate area of Titchfield. However, the finding of a Jade axe head and a flint sickle strongly suggests that some occupational activity may have occurred in the area. A number of axe heads have been found in this country which have been formed from a stone which is geologically grouped as Jade or Jadeite, and have been identified as a raw material which originated from sources outside of Britain. Archaeologists now consider that these rare artefacts were of great significance to our Neolithic ancestors, and that they had no labour utilisation functions. It would seem that they were considered as status items or as religious or dedicational offerings. A beautiful example of a Jade axe head was found carefully placed together with a fine unutilised example of a flint axe head underneath the oldest man-made roadway in Britain, which is the wooden 'Sweet Track' fashioned and laid by Neolithic people across the wetlands in the County of Somerset. These two artefacts are displayed, together with other items related to the 'Sweet Track' discovery, in the County Museum at Taunton.

A temporal division which follows the 'Neolithic' period is known as the 'Bronze-age', and suggests the first metal using groups of people. These Bronze-age ancestors still relied to a large extent on the use of stone and flint tools with which to carry out their daily work requirements. Published records suggest that Bronze working artisans travelled about making and distributing their crafts in various areas of Britain. Many finds have been made which are referred to as Bronze Hoards, where a collection of, often broken, bronze artefacts have been grouped together, presumably with the intention of melting them down and recasting them. A probable 'Bronze Hoard' which consisted of a spear head and seven bronze axe heads has been recorded as having been found at Titchfield.

The divisions which have been given to the Stone-age are arbitrary and for convenience. It is possible that some of these designated divisions may have overlapped each other or have resulted following widely intervening time gaps. Archaeological research is progressing, and new ideas and the science of dating the past continues at a pace that no one would have suspected a few decades ago. A prediction is suggested that by the next time Titchfield History Society decide to produce a new edition of their Book, this Section will be offered by someone having access to a much greater wealth of academic knowledge.

(1) Draper.J.C. 1951. Stone Industries from Rainbow Bar, Hants. Archaeological Newsletter *3*, (9): 147-9

(2) Hack.B. 2008. Rainbow Bar: Suggestions for Early Dating. Hampshire Field Club and Archaeological Society. Newsletter 50, Autumn 2008, 18-19.

Brian Hack.

LATE IRON AGE/ROMANO BRITISH SITE AT UPPER SEGENSWORTH

Following a development application to Fareham Borough Council, the land associated with the Great Barn at Titchfield has been subjected to an archaeological survey in 2008, undertaken by Wessex Archaeology. The result of this survey has not been published, but it has been reported by English Heritage that resulting from this survey, there is "evidence for a Later Iron Age and Romano-British (LIARB) Ditched Settlement within the northwest corner of the site". The map below (Fig. 1.) shows the approximate location of the settlement in the corner of the Great Barn site, alongside the medieval ponds of Carron Row.

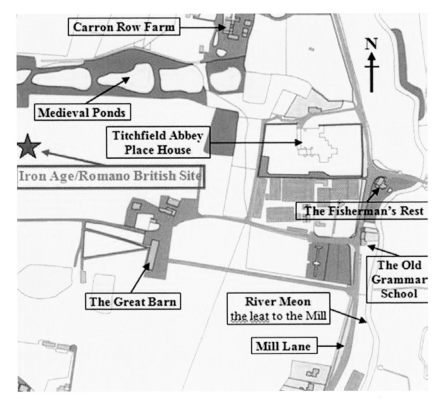

There are, to date, no details of what has been found to substantiate the identification of a LIARB Settlement, but it is fair to assume that a significant enough number of artefacts were found during the archaeological survey. These artefacts would have included some of the following:- pottery shards, tools and weapons, beads and adornments, rudimentary building materials, remains of edible animals (bones and shells) and other corrosion-resistant debris associated with communal living. It is unlikely that any human remains have been found at this site, so far, as such a discovery would have necessitated an immediate full-scale investigation. English Heritage also emphasise that the discovery of a LIARB Settlement in the Tertiary geologies of the Hampshire basin is rare.

Initial Historic Assessment

Fig. 3

The site of the Settlement is where one would expect to find Late Iron Age remains. Atop a hill, with views to Portsdown Hill and the Forest of Bere, the Isle of Wight would be visible from the top of a high point, and probably the Solent. Thus, potential invaders could be identified and communication would be possible with friendly neighbours. Fig.2. shows a view, from the LIARB Settlement site, of the village of Catisfield on the upper right, and Portsdown Hill in the far distance on the upper left, with the top of the ruins of Place House just below. Some of the filled-in trench positions remaining from the archaeological survey carried out by Wessex Archaeology are seen in the foreground.

Adjacent is a fresh water stream, which was used, with great effect, by the medieval monks of Titchfield Abbey, to create their 'running water system' with the pond complex as the 'header tank'. This stream exits into the River Meon just north of Stony Bridge which, it is postulated, was the high-tide mark of the Meon Estuary 2000 years ago and the first fordable point on the river. There would have been food in abundance, to augment the availability of fish, shellfish and sea birds from the river estuary, the Forest of Bere would have provided a rich supply of animals to hunt, and the proximity of the heathland to the west (now Titchfield Common and Locksheath) would have been ideal for grazing for their goats, sheep, swine and cattle. The 1610 map shows Swannycke Heath in the very near vicinity.

The possibility of a LIARB Settlement completely changes our interpretation of the early history of Titchfield. The origins could now be Celtic and not Jute/Saxon, as previously thought. It is easy to see the Romano-British people, following the departure of the Roman legions, descending from their hilltop fortification to be nearer to the river. Were they already Christian, and was there a religious or secular establishment on the site of the Abbey; a suggestion discussed in the past? Did they move along the river and build a mill which would have encouraged silt build-up and the recession, downstream, of the high-water point? Did they form a village near to where St. Wilfred came to build his church? Were they engulfed by the marauding Jutes heading from west Sussex, or the Solent?

In our book *Titchfield A History* there is reference to Tidic's barrow (tidiceshlaewe) near Segensworth, mentioned in the tenth century. Our new find is near Segensworth, and could be described as "Upper Segensworth". Was Tidic a Celt, and might it have been pronounced as a soft 'ch' instead of a hard 'ck'? Or maybe it was 'tch' and the original Titchfield was Tiditchfield? Tidic's barrow may be a Celtic burial site, the location of which is unknown.

It is essential, for Titchfield, that every effort is made to ensure that the most rigorous archaeological excavations possible are carried out to establish the validity of this most important site.

We must hope, that in due course, funds will be found to excavate this fascinating site.   **Ken Groves**

CROFTON OLD CHURCH

Crofton Old Church is without doubt the oldest surviving building in Stubbington. Set some way back from the Titchfield road, it is adjacent to what was the Crofton Manor Hotel on one side and to the cemetery on the other. Until recent times the main Stubbington to Titchfield Road ran past its front gate but major road works of the 1970s redirected this road and today Crofton Old Church lies hidden behind a row of modern houses which form Lychgate Green. Despite all the changes that have occurred around it, Crofton Old Church looks much the  same as it has done for the last 250 years and it still retains its tranquil atmosphere and picturesque beauty.

For some seven centuries a yew tree stood at the west end of the church yard. Sadly, by 1981 the trunk had become so badly decayed that it became necessary to fell the tree in order to prevent it from collapsing on to the main roof of the Church. The remaining wood was then used by Mr Derek George to make crosses and pendants, a fitting end to such a lovely old tree.

The earliest reference to Crofton Old Church is to be found in the Domesday Book of 1087 but it is almost certain that the Anglo-Saxons had a Church on this site. Over the centuries various parts have been added to the building and any visitor is greeted by a collection of tiled roofs all at different angles.

The Church is known by two names. The entry in the Domesday Book is Holy Rood, while a charter of 1331 refers to the church as the chapel of St Edmund. However, the reference is Holy Rood in the Liber Regis, the King's book, of about 1534. A third name of St Thomas is to be found in the Kelly's Directory of Hampshire for 1859 and 1867. This however, may well be a mistake.

Various suggestions have been put forward as to why there seems to be this difference. Some have suggested that Holy Rood was the name given by the Normans whilst St Edmund's is an older name used by the Saxons. This theory is supported by the fact that St Edmund is known to have been an English Saint in the time of the Saxons. Another suggestion is that Holy Rood was its official name while St Edmund's was the name given to the church by the local people of the time. Today, it is usually just referred to as 'the Old Church'. In 1232 Titchfield Abbey was founded by a group of Premonstratensian Canons under Peter des Roches, the Bishop of Winchester. The Charter no longer exists but the Abbey claimed that the bishop had given them the parish Church of the Blessed Peter the Apostle at Titchfield with its chapels of Crofton and Chark. In 1282 permission was given by the Pope for a Canon to serve in the Church of Titchfield.

In 1331 the Abbot (John de Combe) was already Rector of Crofton Chapel as part of the 1232 foundation charter. Elias de Charleton and Benedicta his wife were lords of the manor of Crofton, and had also shown a close interest in the chapel, presumably paying for the secular priest at their own expense. They now gave the *manor* to the Abbey, effectively as a chantry for their souls (and that of King Edward II, who had died in 1327). In return for that gift, the Abbey was to provide the secular priest, and one of the Canons of the Abbey was to conduct a daily service. Having concluded that agreement the Abbot then gave the manor back to Elias and Benedicta for their lifetimes, to revert to him on their deaths (he had royal permission to hold the estate in mortmain – "the dead hand of the church"). A statute of mortmain is property held by an ecclesiastical body or corporation which is not permitted to b sold or transferred. One of the conditions of this grant was that a divine service should be taken by a Canon of the Abbey everyday for the soul of Edward II and also for the souls of Elias and Benedicta after their deaths. The agreement also stipulated that there should not be any change to the normal Sunday or Holy Day services and that the chantry of matins, mass and vespers should be continued by a secular priest as before.

A chantry is a sum of money (endowment) given to a church to provide for priests to pray or conduct religious services, usually for the soul of the giver. After the agreement was reached and witnessed, copies of this charter were retained by Elias and the Abbey. Another copy, written in French, was hung in Crofton Old Church itself. Entries were recorded in the registers of the Bishop of Winchester, the Archbishop of Canterbury and the Royal Chancery.
During their lifetime Elias and Benedicta carried out, at their own expense and discretion, a number of enlargements and repairs to the church at Crofton but after their deaths this responsibility fell once again on to the Abbey.

Colin Prestidge and Gary Willcocks

On 28th December 1537 Titchfield Abbey and its estates were surrendered to King Henry VIII. Two days later, on the 30th, ownership passed to the first Earl of Southampton, Thomas Wriothesley.

Although connections with the Abbey ceased, Crofton Old Church continued to be part of the parish of Titchfield and services at Crofton were taken by curates appointed by the Vicar of St Peter's. A document of the 16th century tells us that the church at Crofton was a Chapel of Ease with Titchfield as its mother church.

Crofton continued to be served by Titchfield until the 14th January 1871 when it became a separate ecclesiastical parish together with Stubbington, Hill Head and Lee-on-the-Solent. The latter eventually became a parish in its own right in 1928.

The first incumbent appointed to the living by the Bishop of Winchester was the Revd Herbert Alder BA who became Vicar of Crofton in 1871. In 1874 the Revd Pitt Cobbett became vicar and in 1878 a new Church of Holy Rood was built in Stubbington Village centre.

The Church itself consists of a chancel, a south chapel, north and south transepts and a nave but there are no aisles. The walls of the church are rendered with sand and cement and buttresses, added at a later date, give additional support. The colour of the original brick has been blended with stone facing and flint. Inside all the walls have been preserved by the old tradition of whitewashing. At the west end of the Church is a turret constructed of board in which is hung a bell, cast by Clement Tosier, dated 1710.

The oldest parts of the Church are the chancel, with its south chapel, and the north transept. These are thought to be early fourteenth century. The walls here are no thicker than two feet, something unusual for buildings of this time. The east window of the chancel has two lights and was damaged by a bomb in World War Two and also by streams of tanks rumbling along the road outside on their way to Normandy in June 1944. After much painstaking work the window has been successfully restored. On either side of this window are wooden panels bearing the Ten Commandments, the Apostle's Creed and the Lord's Prayer in gold and red lettering.

The north transept is rather stumpy in appearance and still retains the original timbers of its roof. From here a door covered in purple felt leads into a small, relatively modern vestry which has been built adjoining the north transept. This vestry has a small window and door which opens out onto the grass.

An ancient feature of the north transept is a leper's squint. This small window was only visible from the outside and has long been bricked up. Any evidence that might remain from the inside was concealed behind a plaque.

The nave, with its square headed windows, was probably built in the fifteenth century. However, a report by architect Richard Halsey dated the 6th August 1980 suggests that the nave, although much altered, is essentially early 12th century (if not the church mentioned in the Domesday Book). Incorporated in the north wall are a number of circa 1100 window heads and he states that the chancel and transepts appear to have been added to the nave rather than vice versa.

There are also substantial pieces of cut stone, some moulded, around the west end and north wall which Halsey believes were brought from the ruins of Titchfield Abbey. The 15th century dating of the nave is possibly based upon the square headed windows, which could themselves be enlargements of earlier openings.

Crofton Old Church by Anne Tout

Interestingly, the nave is not on the same axis as the chancel. Some have said that this feature, found in many medieval churches, is intended to represent the way Christ's head hung on the cross. The west wall of the nave is Georgian and has a three light window with a flat Tudor style mullion.

The roof of the nave is supported by four irregular beams of oak with fifty supporting battens on either side and is of queenpost construction. The roof of the nave is in a poor condition in places and in the past large areas of missing plaster have revealed the underneath rafters. In one particular place chinks of daylight were clearly visible. On occasions it has been necessary to close off certain pews to prevent falling plaster from hitting members of the congregation. Thankfully, the last ten years has seen some restoration of this roof.

The large south transept is a considerably later addition, being built most probably in the mid- eighteenth century and is of poor Gothic style. Like the nave, the south transept has also had plaster missing from its roof. A door leads from the south transept to the chapel and along the south wall are two large windows each with three lights. Situated between these two windows is a large ornate white marble monument dedicated to Thomas Missing who died at

Stubbington on 6th July 1733. In the classical manner of the 18th century the monument is topped by a bust of Thomas, flanked by classical urns and with his coat of arms (see page 113).

A very long epitaph tells us that during his lifetime he had been a merchant and contractor for the provisioning of Gibraltar before becoming a Member of Parliament for Southampton in 1722. Both his son and his grandson became Recorders of Romsey. Thomas Missing, who apparently put up the money for the building of the south transept, was a wealthy gent and at his death was the possessor of a large fortune acquired by honest abilities.

All the window glass in the Church is relatively modern except for the red and gold glass in the window to the right of the vestry door in the north transept. This glass dates back to the 1700s. The glass in the window above the vestry door was given in memory of the daughter of Thomas Naghten of Crofton House. On either side of this door are memorial plaques to various members of the Naghten family. One plaque is for Thomas himself while the other plaques are in memory of his sons. Outside in the graveyard, to the north-east of the chancel, are also several graves (mainly female) belonging to this illustrious family.

In the nave is a stone font which probably dates back to the fifteenth century. A short stem supports an octagonal bowl lined with lead. The pulpit is late seventeenth century and has panels of oak.

Laid in the floor of the chancel is a stone in memory of James Mill who died in 1806. A plaque close to the Communion table is in memory of the Reverend David Haynes who died on 7th May 1849, aged 55. David Haynes was Curate in charge at Crofton for 11 years. Another plaque in the chancel was given by Henry Blackwood in memory of his wife Elizabeth who died on 30th October 1802, aged 23.

In the chapel is a large Bible and prayer book. These were given in 1865 by the Revd Philip Thresher MA on completion of restoration work at Crofton. At that time the Revd Walter Cosser was Vicar and the Revd William Foster of Stubbington House School was Curate.

Dotted around the Church are various other plaques. In the south transept is a plaque in memory of John Guitton who died on 4th December 1855, aged 78, while in the north wall of the nave is a memorial plaque given by the wife of Lord Henry Paulet. Lord Henry died on 28th January 1932, aged 64. At the west end of the nave are three plaques in memory of the o'Bryen family and they include one in memory of Rear Admiral Edward o'Bryen who died on Christmas Day 1808, aged 54. The Rear Admiral must have been a distinguished gentleman for he served as Flag Captain aboard HMS Monarch and fought in the famous battle of Camperdown on 11th October 1797.

The Chapelry of Crofton, which had been part of the ancient parish of Titchfield for 800 years, and which included Stubbington and Lee-on-the-Solent, became a separate parish in 1871. But the ancient church was too small for the growing population of the area, and in 1876 a new church was built at Stubbington, also called Holy Rood. Lee-on-the-Solent in turn became separate in 1930. The Old Church at Crofton was for many years used only as a mortuary chapel and its structure deteriorated.

In the first half of the twentieth century the Old Church became increasingly used. In 1963 electric light and heating were installed, and in 1982 the Friends of Old Crofton Church were constituted. Since then about £500,000 has been raised towards the maintenance of the building. A first phase of restoration work was undertaken in 1994, and has gone on. Continued problems with the roof required localised repairs to cure leaks and maintain odd rafters and beams. This work culminated in 2007 with the stripping of the whole roof, the nave and north transept being taken down to bare rafters. The roof was then refelted, retiled and lime plastered. An anonymous donation allowed the west window to be replaced with a stone surround instead of the original wooden frame. In 2005-6 a toilet and small utility room were built on. The leper squint has been reopened by the removal of a memorial. During all of this work, including the stripping of the roof, church services continued as normal.

The church, now known as St. Edmund's, has returned to being an integral part of Stubbington parish, and its more traditional style of service complements that at Holyrood. The church is administered, and services are conducted, by the parish team based at Holyrood. Since 1996 the number of services has increased. These services attract a worshipping congregation numbered in the seventies. At Christmas there is a service of nine lessons and carols and nativity services which altogether have attracted over 360 worshippers. The church is open to visitors on the 18th of each month between 10.00 am and 12 noon.

It is heartening, in this increasingly secularised world, to see how the efforts of a small group of devoted and hardworking individuals can lead to the revival of an historic little church like Old Crofton.

Colin Prestidge and Gary Willcocks

TITCHFIELD ABBEY: ITS FOUNDATION AND IT'S ABBOTS.

A Premonstratensian abbey was founded at Titchfield in 1232 by Peter des Roches, bishop of Winchester. It was in existence for 300 years, being surrendered to the Crown in 1538 during the Dissolution of the Monasteries. The list of abbots which follows, taken from the manuscripts of the abbey, was printed in the Victoria County History in 1903; dates have been added and some additions made by Howard Colvin and by the present writer.

RICHARD, the first abbot, came from Halesowen with his brethren in the year 1222(1232), and ruled this church well and religiously. He died on 16 June, and was buried before the door of the chapter-house.

1232-1238

ISAAC was the second abbot; in his time the manors of Cadlands and Inkpen were acquired. He died on 19 June, and was buried in the cloister before the door of the chapter-house, on the right hand of the monument of the first abbot.   1239-1259

After his death, HENRY DE BRAN WYK succeeded him. He was afterwards sought as abbot of Halesowen, and there rested in peace.

1259-1265

To him, HENRY DE SPERSHOLTE succeeded, in whose time the manor of Newland was acquired and lost. He died on 22 September, and was buried in the cloister. 1265-1272/3

To him succedeed BROTHER IVO, in whose time the manor of Mirabel was acquired and lost. He died on 3 March and was buried in the cloister.   1272-1275

ADAM, the third? abbot of this church, ruled with honour. He died on 14

September, and was buried in the cloister on the left of the monument to Abbot Peter de Wynton. 1276-1289

WILLIAM DE BYKETON, the fourth abbot, was a venerable ruler of the church; he died on 8 November, and was buried in the church, at the altar of St. Richard. 1289-1303/4

JOHN SYDEMANTON, fifth abbot, ruled well, and died on 3 December. He was buried in the cloister, between the door of the library on the south and the monument of Abbot Wynton on the north. 1304-1308/9

ROGER DE CANDEVER, sixth abbot, ruled this church honourably and religiously for about eighteen years. He died on 5 August, and was buried in the cloister at the entrance to the church near the altar of St. Peter.
1308/9-1328

JOHN DE COMBE, seventh abbot, in whose time the manors of Crofton and Fontelegh-Pageham were acquired. He ruled this church for about twenty years, and died on 5 May, and was buried in the cloister, at the head of the monument of Abbot Roger de Candever. 1328-1348

PETER DE WYNTON, eighth abbot, ruled this house religiously for one year and six months. He died on 16 July, and was buried in the cloister between the monument of Abbot Adam on the north and Abbot Sydemanton on the south. 1348-1349

WILLIAM DE WALLOP, ninth abbot, ruled this church in the best possible way for twenty years, nine months and three days. In his time the land and tenement of Markes and Brykoresland were acquired and appropriated. He also acquired, but did not appropriate, the land and tenement of Ward, the land of Froghemour, the land of Firsteburyesland at Chirk, and the tenements which were John Goudale's in Titchfield. Also in his days John Edindon gave his manor of Portsea and Copenore to the priory. He died on 23 May, and was buried in the cloister, north of the monument of Abbot Candever. 1349-1370

JOHN DE THORNI, tenth abbot, ruled prudently over this church for nineteen years, thirteen weeks and five days; in his time the lands and tenements mentioned under his predecessor were all appropriated. He died on 20 September, and was buried in the cloister at the feet of the image of the Blessed Virgin, which he had erected there in honour of the Mother of God by
1370-1390.

JOHN DE ROMSEY, eleventh abbot of this church, ruled honourably.
1390-1410?

A missing name? 1410-1420?

23

RICHARD AUBREY   1420-142?

THOMAS BENSTEADE, the thirteenth abbot ruled well, and resigned his staff under compulsion.   1440-1440?

WILLIAM WINCHESTOUR, ALIAS FRYER, was fourteenth abbot, and ruled six and a half years.   1460-146?

WILLIAM AUYTEN, fifteenth abbot, ruled the church well for sixteen years. He built the house commonly called The Grete Place. He also restored the windows of all the chambers, and built another house near the cross in the body of the town. He died on 25 October, and was buried near the monument of John Thorny.   1466-146?

THOMAS BLANKPAYN, seventeenth abbot, ruled for twenty-one years, and resigned on a pension.   1493-151?

The REV. FATHER JOHN, Bishop of Elphin in Ireland, abbot in commendam of Welbeck and Titchfield, prebendary of York and Southwell and visitor of the Premonstratensian Order, the eighteenth abbot, rebuilt the ruined church.
1515-153?

JOHN SALISBURY   1536-1537

The list seems to be a compilation of notes made by different writers at irregular intervals throughout the 300 years of the abbey's existence. This has resulted in several anomalies. The names of the first five abbots are followed by Adam the third and then the numbering continues to an eighteenth abbot. Adam was said to have been the abbot, buried near the monument to the future Peter de Wynton; in fact, Peter's monument had been erected near the existing grave of Adam - but 60 years later. Long gaps in the early fifteenth century suggest that there may be a name missing. Later, in the confusion of the process of the abbey's dissolution, the list ends abruptly with John Salisbury, but is incomplete. Another abbot, John Simpson, had preceded Salisbury, but had been appointed and resigned within a few months, in 1536. It was John Salisbury, Bishop of Thetford, who surrendered the abbey to the Crown, on 28th December 1537. It was immediately acquired by Thomas Wriothesley. There was what was almost certainly a clerical error in this list, giving 1222 and not 1232 for the arrival of Abbot Richard. But an attempt to clarify this error leads us from a modern mistake to a medieval muddle: for Titchfield Abbey was founded twice!

In August 1231 King Henry III (he was 23) gave to Peter des Roches the church of Titchfield, with its lands and properties, for the foundation of a house of religion, not of the Premonstratensian order, but of the order of the canons of St. Augustine, the Augustinians. The grant was of the parish church and its lands, which we can assume included the farm in the Middle Ages, called the Rectory Barton, now Fernhill Farm, the site of the great barn. The intention may have been that the Augustinians would build their monastery there.

The Abbott's Graves

A few days later, another royal document repeated this grant, this time to the Augustinians who had been brought to refound a religious house at Titchfield, an apparent reference to the minster community we know to have existed there before the Norman Conquest and possibly later. So the Augustinians (seemingly from Bristol), taking possession of the church though not of the manor, had arrived - but not stayed. For, just two months later, in October 1231, the situation was changed. Yet another royal document now granted to Peter des Roches not only the church and its lands but the manor itself, a much larger and more valuable acquisition, for the foundation of an unspecified religious house. The bishop was changing his mind. It may be that amongst the manorial lands was a site with a better water supply than any on the church lands -

the present site of Place House. Why Peter decided that the Augustinians were not suitable to develop this site we shall never know. But after a year's consideration and no doubt negotiation, in September 1232 the King again granted the manor to the bishop, this time specifically for the foundation of an abbey of canons of the Premonstratensian Order. By then Abbot Richard and his brethren may already have arrived. So if in future an event should be organised to celebrate the abbey's foundation we can safely take it to have been on 20th September 1232.

Victoria County History: Hampshire III. 1903: The White Canons in England, H.M.Colvin, 1951: Calendar of Charter Rolls. 1226-1257. pgs.139,163: Calendar of Close Rolls. 1227-1231 p.572; BL Add 70506, f214a.

Stonework detail in St Peter's Norman Doorway

George Watts

A CHAPEL FOR HOOK? - A MEDIEVAL DISPUTE

The hamlet of Hook (Hamelhoke) at the mouth of the Hamble river was mentioned in Domesday Book. The survey recorded that Hook was valued as one hide, and there was one plough in lordship and one in the hands of five tenants, perhaps 240 acres of land in all. There were three slaves, a meadow of one acre, and woodland worth one pig. This small manor was valued at 25 shillings.By the fourteenth century the people of Hook were fishermen and boat builders, and as coastal and international trade developed Hook fleet and the Hamble river provided a secure and convenient anchorage for merchant ships, where they could pay the taxes due to Southampton and save the long tack up Southampton Water.

Fig 1

Hook port was also convenient for travellers to the continent and on coastal journeys by sea, often shorter than on the poor roads of that time. The monks of Netley Abbey on visits to Titchfield would land at Hook, and the Abbot of Titchfield would leave from Hook to visit Southampton and his manor at Cadland. As royal ships were moored in the river, there would have been regular visitors on naval business. In April 1378 Richard Earl of Arundel met William Montagu, Earl of Salisbury at Hamelhoke to agree a dowry of 500 marks for the marriage of Richard's daughter to William's son and heir. They were both Admirals of the West and South, and Richard was about to embark for Harfleur, which he attacked at Whitsun 1378.

.

In the 14th century Hook was divided between two manors which were held under separate lordships, Hook Valence - West Hook, and Hook Mortimer - East Hook. Both manors, together with Brownwich, were acquired by Thomas Wriothesley after the Dissolution of the Monasteries.

The two Hook manors were held by Roger Mortimer, second Earl of March, until his death in 1360, and in August 1354 King Edward III granted him a weekly Monday market, and an annual fair on 24th June. The grant provided that ships with merchandise, excepting wool, might trade at the port of Hook, paying the customs due to the port of Southampton. The market would be popular, for with the usual market produce there might be merchandise from the ships in the port. Customers would come from nearby villages and by boat from villages on the Hamble and along the coast. The trade might be of imports of wine, oil, grain and iron, or more exotic items from Genoa or Venice such as silk, Turkish cotton, spices and wax. Exports might include shellfish, salt, and hides, and wool and cloth by licence.

Houses at Hook at that time would have two rooms, with perhaps an annexe for animals. The main room would have a central fire on the earth floor, with smokeholes in the roof. The house would be thatched and timber framed, with wattle and daub walls with wood shutters on the windows. Hook was evidently a prosperous centre with resident merchants and ship owners, and the people felt confident enough to build their own chapel. It was an ambitious project, not long after the Black Death of 1348-49.

A wealthy Southampton merchant, William Mapull, gave land for the chapel. He had a house at Hook, for which in 1381 he paid the rent of 1s. a year. He was mayor of Southampton four times and also burgess of Parliament four times, so held a position of authority with powerful connections. As Mayor and Admiral of Southampton he was responsible for the jurisdiction of the ports between Portsmouth and Lymington which paid harbour dues to Southampton. William Mapull was a man of some standing both in Southampton and the City of London, where he was a freeman. In 1397 he was wealthy enough to loan £20.00 to Richard II (nearly £10,000 today), so he was in the position to call in favours on behalf of the chapel. He might also have contributed when 'The mayor, bailiff and the good men of Southampton' lent Richard 11170 marks (over £55,000 today).

The Bishop's register of 15th March 1364 recorded: Pope Urban Vth at Avignon had received a petition from the inhabitants of Hook to erect a chapel because of the flooding of the pond on the road and the distance to the parish church at Titchfield. In bad weather many cannot get to church, many cannot receive the sacraments when sick, and children die without baptism. The Pope ordered Bishop William Edington to consult the rector of the parish church of Titchfield on the erection of a chapel at Hook, and also to enquire into an endowment for a chaplain to serve the chapel, while still preserving the rights of the parish church.

There was probably some substance in this claim, as in 1393 Richard II's baggage cart was said to have been obstructed, probably by the pond at Fleet End. The King and Queen Anne were on progress from Beaulieu to Titchfield. An extract from the 14th century Abbey Register states that the highway was in a ruinous condition by reason of the overflowing of the water of a certain fishery, which the Abbots of Titchfield were at times beyond memory to repair. However Bishop Edington died in 1367 and his successor Bishop William of Wykeham took time to consider the Pope's instruction. In July 1374 the new Pope Gregory XI instructed the Bishop to enquire into the proper construction and endowment of the chapel at Hamelhoke and a suitable person to its cure. This was at the request of John duke of Lancaster, Thomas earl of Warwick, Hugh earl of Stafford, William earl of Suffolk and Edward le Despencer, lord of the place. Hook had entered the realm of high politics.

The inhabitants of Hook, impatient after the ten year wait, must have taken this as permission, and built the chapel in c.1377-8 without the authority of the Bishop. All the inhabitants would probably have contributed to the chapel in kind or money, according to their means. An example would be the gifts received for the funds to rebuild Bodmin Church at a similar time: old timber, an old coffer, a cow, lambs and a goose, an old chandelier, wages for a day's work at the quarry, gifts of money, stones for the church, roof spars, tiles, old iron, and a year's salary from the vicar.

Hook was in the ancient parish of Titchfield, and the Abbot of Titchfield, John de Thorny, indignant at the flouting of the Bishop's authority and concerned at his loss of revenue from the offices provided by the parish church of Titchfield, complained to the Bishop.

On the 23rd December 1377 the Bishop informed John Langrysshe, his representative, that an illegal chapel had been built at the hamlet of Hoke without permission, and parishioners did not attend their parish church and instead celebrated mass in their own chapel. They had rung bells to summon people to church. They had unlawful use of a font, and they no longer gave offerings and tithes to Titchfield. This behavior endangered their souls and scandalised many people. The Bishop, wishing to provide for the indemnity of the church, and to meet the dangers to the souls of our flock orders John Langrysshe to warn the parishioners and chaplain of Hook three times publicly that within twelve days they must cease these activities and make amends to church and clergy, or they will be excommunicated and the chapel placed under an interd'ict.

John Langrysshe reported: The people of Hook had continued to celebrate mass in their chapel. He had attended mass in a crowded Titchfield church, and announced the Bishop 's ruling. This provoked uproar, and the people of Hook shouted that they would keep their chapel and divine offices, without contradiction from anyone.

On the 18th January 1378 the Bishop placed the matter in the hands of Archdeacon Edyndone, John de Lydeford and the official John de Campedon. On the 22nd January John de Lydeford held a sitting in St. Mary Overy Southwark: He suspended Hook chapel and pronounced an interdict, and he ordered the main offenders to appear before the Bishop at Winchester on the Thursday after Palm Sunday, to hear their charges. They did not appear and instead lodged an appeal and then two further appeals, one on 5th March which was fixed to the door of Winchester Cathedral, and the third on 17th March in London. They were refused.

The dean of Droxford learnt that despite the interdict the inhabitants of Hook had employed a chaplain Robert Whelere to hear Mass and other offices, so on the orders of the Bishop, pronounced excommunication on William Mapull and his supporters.

Excommunication was pronounced upon:

William Mapull	John Mapull	Henry Kyne
John Tolle	John Wyrng	Robed Scottere
William Tolle	Richard Tukkere	Richard Suttone
John Fordere	Peter Fysshe	William Gadales
Henry Northwell	John Digelle	John Tollere
John Boukeswell	John Baysse	John Aubrey
Robed Malgere	Roger atte Mere	Richard Chaumpeneye
John Pipe	John Laurens	William Webbe
William Waryn	Dm. Robert Whelere, chaplain.	

There is a reference to a further penalty of 1000 marks for William Maple and Henry Kyne, which appears to be in the event of a breach in an agreement. On the 29th January 1378 William Mapull, aggrieved and angry, wrote to the new Pope Urban VI: he repeated the points about the djfficulty of travel to Titchfield and the loss of church offices, but added the dangerous possibility of invasion when the parishioners were at church in Titchfield. He referred to the lord of Hamelhoke, who with the parishioners, had been prepared to fund a priest to be able to receive sacraments and to provide a font necessary for the baptism of children.

They had also guaranteed that they would continue to support the mother church with all the rights and emoluments for ever. The Bishop had refused to listen to their petition, so having sufficient authority they had built the chapel. The Bishop however warned the parishioners with threatening letters to close the chapel, although no legal summons had been made, and pronounced a monition despite their legitimate appeal to the Pope. No copy of the monition had been received despite repeated requests to be able to consult counsel, and they were unjustly excommunicated. He had not been to Winchester Cathedral, the correct place for appeals because of the fear of ambush by his enemies, and the bishop would not appoint another place. He and his adherents felt they been unjustly oppressed, and threw themselves upon the protection of the Apostolic See.

Norden's Map showing the chapel

William Mapull's claims of danger were probably exaggerated, but many people would have been shocked at his refusal to accede to the bishop's ruling.
By 1400 William Mapull had died. Believing that permission from the Pope was sufficient, and in defiance of the bishop, the residents or Hook continued to worship in their chapel.

When hearing of this on the 31st May 1400 the Bishop ordered four clerks of the diocese of Winchester, the dean of Droxford, the rector of Rowner and the vicars of Fareham and Titchfleld to inhibit William Cake the chaplain from celebrating divine offices, and the inhabitants of Hook from hearing them. If the chaplain disobeys, he is to appear at St.Mary Overy, Southwark on the 19th June to answer the charges and be punished.

On the 10th June the dean of Droxford went in person to Hook and was met by the residents led by the chaplain William Cake, William Warren, William Dageney and William Prymer, who violently resisted him with drawn bows and arrows, and threatened him with death if he demanded the execution of the mandate, and William Prymer seized the mandate with daring impudence and kept possession of it. In fear for his life the dean did not dare to inhibit them, and the chaplain could not be apprehended. The matter remained unresolved, and the people of Hook continued to worship in their chapel.

The Abbot John de Romsey then referred the matter to the Court of Canterbury, who ordered the four clerks to serve further inhibitions on William Cake and the residents, but were again thwarted with threats, and the summons that they should appear at the Court of Arches could not be served.

After discussions with the Court of Canterbury the Abbot decided to treat with the executors of William Mapull, John Mycol of London, John Batour rector of Sherbome St. John, William Tabeller of Clopham and Hugh Champion of Southampton.

Agreement on terms and conditions were reached on 16th November 1400; but they became null and void because the Bishop would not give his assent. On 31st December 1401 Pope Boniface IX wrote to all the inhabitants of the town of Hamelette Hoke at their petition, and at the petition of the executors of William Mapull. They will depute an ordained priest to celebrate masses for the soul of William Mapull and themselves, with licence to hear confessions, grant absolution, baptize children and give extreme unction, saving the rights of the parish church. This was copied to the Archbishop of Canterbury, and the Bishops of London and Salisbury.

This prompted the Archbishop of Canterbury Thomas Arundel to demand to know from the Abbot why the Pope's instructions should not be implemented. The Bishop replied that the Titchfield church was already supporting two chapels, and the Hook chapel had been erected illegally and was under an interdict, but that despite that for more than a year John Mycol, an executor of William Mapull, was having mass celebrated there.

On 6th July 1402, for the sake of peace, the abbot, John Mycoll and the inhabitants made an agreement through mediation, and the abbot appointed Brother Geoffrey Bicton as proctor to act on his behalf.

1. The executors must pay ten marks annually for a chaplain approved by the bishop. If they cease payment, the abbot is not bound to maintain a chaplain until the sum is paid in full with arrears and expenses. The chapel is suspended from mass and no other chaplain may celebrate there under pain of excommunication.

2. If the abbot fails to provide a chaplain after the payment of ten marks, he must pay twenty marks to the bishop.

3. The abbot is not responsible for any expenses other than the chaplain.

4. The abbot can dismiss the chaplain if he performs outside the agreement. The chaplain should only say mass in a low voice and no other office. He may give the sick and bedridden consecrated bread and wine on Sundays, unless otherwise ordered. He may only celebrate mass with a portable altar as if in a private chapel.

5. The clerk of the parish church will continue to visit parishioners with holy water and receive his accustomed fee.

6. The inhabitants of Hook must continue to support their parish church for repair of the building and fencing when necessary, and can be compelled to do this by church tax.

7. On the four principal feasts of the Church the chaplain is to say mass in Titchfield parish church for the soul of William Mapull.

8. Villeins tied to the Abbey are excluded from the agreement lest they should claim to be free.

9. The executors and inhabitants are to renounce all apostolic letters past and future, and to hand them to the abbot.

10. No other priest may celebrate without separate licence. (Unless in the presence of an important person, such as a King, Duke, Baron or Knight).

11. When these articles are agreed on both sides through good consideration, the agreement will be confirmed by the Bishop at the expense of the inhabitants.

The reservation regarding exemptions from a separate licence was added knowing that visiting dignitaries would bring their own chaplain. John Mycoll on behalf of the inhabitants of Hook completely refused to agree to these articles.

In response to the Pope's mandate the Archbishop of Canterbury proceeded with the institution of a priest in the chapel, and ordered the abbot to obey the Pope's instructions with threats of penalties for non-compliance, and forbidding him to obstruct the chaplain in celebrating Mass and divine offices.

The abbot appealed against the Archbishop's orders, and proceeded to obtain royal writs to send a representative with an appeal to Rome. However, on the advice of senior counsel, the abbot instead employed a proctor at the papal court and sent a letter with an appeal to Pope Boniface for a revocation of his Bull to the inhabitants. This was between March 1403 and January 1404.

The Abbot John de Romsey wrote indignantly to the Pope: The residents of Hook have been misleading him. Hook is not a town as they have stated but are two hamlets of Hook Valence and Hook Mortimer; also they can travel to Titchfield without danger or dfficulty at any time of the year. The Pope had thought good to grant a full and free licence to the priest and executors of William Mapull deceased, to celebrate masses and divine services for ever. They had however built the chapel and instituted a chaplain without the authority of the Bishop, and by the singular rashness of William Mapull when living, had received the Pope's permission with truth being suppressed and had not told the Pope that the bishop had placed the chapel under interdict in 1379. After repentance they had received absolution, but the interdict had not been released. He also complained that the parish church already had the expense of two other chapels and could not support a third. He beseeched the Pope to revoke his permission for the chapel which had been obtained by malicious corruption and stealth, and was tending to prejudice and grievious damage to the church and to the authority of the Bishop.

The Abbot's entreaty was successful. On 7th June 1404 Pope Boniface IX sent a Bull to the Abbot revoking his permission for a chapel at Hook. There was no necessity for a chapel, and he had not known the chapel had been built without licence from the Bishop and had been placed under an interdict, and his permission had been obtained by deception and with truth suppressed which resulted in prejudice and injury to the abbot. All proceedings past and future are nullified, nevertheless the dispute rumbled on for another 33 years, until finally, it would seem, in November 1437 Pope Eugene IV confirmed to the inhabitants of Hokemortemere that they have mass and other divine offices celebrated by a fit priest in their chapel even on a portable altar saving the rights of their parish church.

There was a further mention of the chapel, when in June 1446 the southern clergy granted Henry IV a subsidy of 6s.8d. from every chaplain who had not been previously assessed for tax. This included the chaplain of Hook Mortimer. By the end of the 15th century the Hundred Years War was over. Henry VII was developing Portsmouth as a naval base, and Southampton was a prosperous trading port. The Hamble River was losing its status as an important, secure harbour. The chapel survived the Reformation when in 1537 Titchfield Abbey was given to Thomas Wriothesley by Henry VIII.

There is a reference on 25th April 1589 to the sale of 'Hook chappell and half an acre adjoining' and on Norden's map of 1595 the chapel is marked as a chapel of ease. In 1611 there is a reference to the "advowson of the churche of Hooke", but it is unlikely that the chapel was still in use. By then the Hook fleet was silting up and became too shallow for the new larger ships. Merchant ships which had enjoyed the convenience of the fleet anchorage moved up river to Hamble and Bursledon, so the population of Hook declined and could not afford to maintain the chapel. There are further references to half an acre of land called Chappell Close until 1720, and in 1785 Arthur Hornby bought the estate, and what remained of the village of Hook moved to a new site.

Pip Leach

I would like to thank Dr Alison Deveson, George Watts, Keith Hayward, Penny Daish, Susan Forer and Paul Cope for their advice and assistance, and to acknowledge the contribution of the late Sally Hall.

Sources:
BL 29/56, m.587/70507, ff148-68.
HRO Wriothesley Deeds, 5M53: 1294: 182: 1044: 1422: 1111/18.
Calendar of Charter Rolls, vol.5, 1341-1417.
Calendar of Papal Rolls, Pope Eugene IV, f230d.
John Lydford's Book, ed. D. M Owen, Devon and Cornwall Record Series 20.
Edington's Register, ed. S. F. Hockey, Hampshire Record Series 8, Pt. 2, no 392, P. 73.
Wykeham's Register, vol.2, pp.281-285.
The Black Book of Southampton, vol.], p.33.
Victoria County History of Hampshire, vol.3, pp.225-228.
Figure 1: Hook and the Fleet in 1610.

1402 agreement; Hampshire Record Office HRO 5M51/182

Richard II and the Fishpond

In the summer of 1393, King Richard II was on a royal progress in southern England. On August 2nd, apparently coming by boat from Beaulieu Abbey, he arrived in Titchfield, landing at Warsash. With him was his first wife, Anne of Bohemia, daughter of the Holy Roman Emperor (she was to die in the following year). They had with them a distinguished retinue, among them the Bishop of Salisbury, the Earl Marshal, the Earl of Rutland, Lord Thomas Percy - the Steward of the Household, and Lord Henry Percy (Shakespeare's future Hotspur), who was Steward of Burgundy.

Richard and Anne

Sadly, this splendid occasion was marred by an unfortunate incident. The boats carrying the party seem to come ashore at what was to become Newtown. The king and the court had ridden round by way of Warsash and Brook, and thence by the *via regia*, the King's Highway, to Titchfield and Titchfield Abbey. But the carriages of the royal baggage train set straight off eastwards. Starting perhaps on the small patch of common land there, they found themselves travelling along tracks, between ditches and banks, and through gates and hurdle fences. Then, after a mile, they unexpectedly came to an impassable obstacle, a large fishpond which was not only steep-sided and deep, but in flood. The baggage train was quite literally stuck.

This fishpond was in the valley, in living memory called Holemore, which runs to the east of the Jolly Farmer Inn towards Fleet End. There is no longer a pond in the valley, just a stream running through a strip of woodland. But the large earthwork dam at the bottom end is still there. The pond was both a fishpond and a millpond. The mill had been built by the Abbot of Titchfield Abbey in the years since the Black Death of 1349 for the use of his local tenants; he had also established a gated path to the mill.

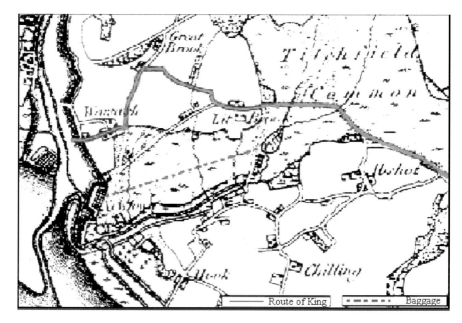

The royal baggage train took some time to find a way out of their tricky situation. Meanwhile the king and queen and the court had arrived at the abbey and were waiting for their baggage. The king, once the young hero of the Peasants' Revolt, was becoming increasingly irascible. The main recipient of the royal comments was probably the Steward of the Household, Lord Thomas, who had allowed the carriages and packhorses of the baggage train to set off across an unfamiliar landscape without consulting anyone, and without scouting ahead.

In due course all was sorted out and there was a great feast at the abbey. Most of the expenses were paid for by Lord Henry, but the abbey contributed twelve fine pike - which might ironically have come from the very same fishpond.

But Lord Thomas did not leave the matter there. When the stay was over, he set up a court in Southampton, and summoned the abbot to answer the charge that he had failed to maintain a highway along the route that the baggage train had taken.

The abbot disputed the charge, and called seven local men to give evidence; they give us, 550 years later, very nice evidence of the character of medieval tenants. They were John Kech of Abshot, aged 68; his son John, aged 22; John Kute aged 66, from the now lost hamlet of Felde; Nicholas Cope, aged 63, of

Titchfield; William Hyrchon, aged 67; John Edmund, aged 72; and John Sweyn, aged 55. They supported their landlord, Abbot John de Romsey. The correct route from Warsash to Titchfield, they said, was the road the king had taken, which ran through the middle of Brook, then eastwards, presumably down Greenaway Lane, to the hamlet of Felde, then through another lost hamlet, Stoford, and on to the Hunte Pond and so to Titchfield. This was the King's Highway, which the abbot had a duty to maintain - and did so. The route taken by the baggage train had never been a road. Their evidence gives

Anne and Richard

us all kinds of detail about that route. Much of the land had once been cultivated but had been neglected since the Black Death;the mistaken route passed through the common field of Brook; they could remember wheat and rye being grown there; they and others had prevented people establishing a right of way there. One particular issue was access to and from the parish church at Titchfield, an issue which also vexed the inhabitants of Hook. They recalled the case of a funeral procession, carrying the body of Robert Page of Warsash, being turned back on to the highway; and another incident in which the great wedding party of Robert Sender's daughter, on her way to the house of her new husband, Walter Wylles, in Warsash, was turned around.

Lord Thomas had found no witnesses to contradict the local evidence; and meanwhile things had moved on; as our account says "the court of the lord king had gone elsewhere" (to Salisbury in fact). The affair of the flooded fishpond had only been a passing irritation to the lords of the Household. To us it gives a fascinating glimpse of English society from king to countryman six centuries ago.

from the Rememoratorium of Titchfield Abbey, BL 29/55, f 122b sq.

George Watts

DATING TITCHFIELD'S BUILDINGS

Several important buildings in Titchfield have recently been dated by dendrochronology (or tree-ring dating) and this has greatly added to their historical interest. Dendrochronology is carried out by analysing samples from oak timbers in an historic building. This produces the precise date, or date-range, at which these timbers were felled. Fortunately, except in rare circumstances, oak was 'green' (or freshly felled) when used so that, within a year or so, we know when a building was erected.

The Abbey Barn

The great Abbey Barn is, at about 46.5m (153' 0") in length, the longest medieval agricultural building in Hampshire to survive intact. The unusual form of its roof timbers is paralleled by only two other Hampshire buildings both of which date to c. 1300. It is a form that shows the influence of Norman-French carpentry; an influence likely to have been felt in the thirteenth century rather than later. Moreover, its great size and fine oak timbers suggest a building date during a time of agricultural plenty. For both these reasons, expert opinion favoured a building-date of c. 1300 for the barn at a time when agriculture was buoyant and thus providing a good income for great lords like the Abbot of Titchfield.

The tree-ring date of 1408/9 was a surprise and produced much scratching of expert heads! Could it be that an enterprising Abbot had overcome a period of financial difficulty by restructuring estate management in such a way as to increase production? Or - more excitingly - could the barn have been intended to store supplies for the invasion of France then being planned by Prince Henry and Henry Beaufort? The invasion was to be launched from nearby Southampton and the Prince would have had the money to subsidise the erection of a large storage building.

The Norman - French style of carpentry at such a late date is also puzzling. Perhaps a Premonstratensian abbey would have had access to French craftsmen and in any case, there was a significant French colony in Southampton. We will probably never know the answers to these intriguing questions.

The original building was entirely timber-framed and would have had smaller entrance doors than at present. In 1560-62, the second Earl of Southampton created two larger entrances with porches and it may be that, at the same time, he replaced part of the outer walls with stone taken from redundant Abbey buildings.

Place House Cottage stands near the entrance to the monastic buildings. From the road it appears to be quite an ordinary brick cottage but at the back, where the River Meon runs through the garden, is some fine timber framing. The southernmost two bays of this framing could date to the mid 16th century but the next two bays had very large, curved timbers (Figure 1). Could these two bays predate the Dissolution of the Abbey and, if so, was this building associated with the Abbey in some way? A tree-ring date of the winter of 1447/48 answered the first question and documentary research went a good way towards answering the second. The two bays of 1447/48 originally comprised one open room with no floors or partitions. There was no evidence of soot on the rafters to indicate that there had once been an open hearth. Whatever the original purpose of this building, it had clearly not been a medieval house. However, the building is called 'The School' on a map of 1753 and it is shown on the famous estate map of 1605-10. When Leland viewed Place House in 1542, he noted 'the grammar school close to the river bank' and, as the Abbey had only been dissolved a few years beforehand, it seems likely that this had been the schoolroom. It is known that the Abbey was a distinguished place of learning and that it was not uncommon for monastic schools to be attached to the almonry at the monastery gate. Such a school, overseen by one of the monks, would provide both training for novices and an education in Latin grammar for boys who did not intend to follow a monastic life..

But why should such a school have been built in or shortly after 1447/48? Henry VI who, as founder of Eton College, clearly had a profound interest in education, was married at Titchfield Abbey in 1445. In 1447, in recognition of the courtesy shown to him by the Abbot and convent, he granted the Abbey various liberties and immunities. It is an intriguing possibility that, as a further mark of his gratitude, he sponsored the foundation of a monastic grammar school.

'The Jetty' 28 South Street

The oldest building that has so far been tree-ring dated in Titchfield is a jettied house on
the east side of South Street, appropriately named 'The Jetty'. Dated to 1412/13, its central timber-frame is remarkable in that it combines both a two-bay open hall and a continuous jetty along the street front. Access between the first-floor chambers on either side of the hall was by means of a gallery. This combination of features in a

medieval house has not been recorded outside Hampshire and, even within the county, has only been found in two 15th century houses in Titchfield and one in Wickham. It would seem that this was a local carpentry innovation that failed to spread.

At the very end of the 15th century open halls began to go out of fashion. The wealthy could afford to build a brick chimney to carry away the smoke from the hall fire. The less wealthy contained the smoke by building a timber-framed partition within the hall, thus creating a so-called 'smoke bay'. This occurred at 'The Jetty' at some time between 1489 and 1521.

Segensworth Farm.

North of the former Abbey and hard against the road leading to Wickham is a long, low out-building belonging to Segensworth Farm. This building is shown on the estate map of 1605-10 and the late Chris Draper seems to have been wrong in supposing that it was only moved to its present site in the 18th century. He was, however, right in saying that it was basically a 15th century structure because dendrochronology has given a felling date-range for its main timbers of 1436-1467. He was also right in observing that it was built as stables with accommodation for a groom at one end. In the 15th century, Segensworth was a small manorial estate and held by an important local family called Wayte. They may have kept farm horses in this building or, quite possibly, their best riding horses. In either case a medieval stable block is a very rare survival and this is the oldest surviving example known in the county.

Great Posbrook was another manor within the great medieval estate of Titchfield. Great Posbrook Farmhouse, a fine building of the late 16th or early 17th century date still survives in part. The great, timber-framed barn belonging to the house is nearly 100 feet in length and has recently been renovated . Dendrochronology caused more problems that it solved for some of the great posts dated to 1579-90 while others dated 1603-35. Clearly the barn could not have been built before the latter date but why had a group of earlier posts been used? These earlier posts had not been re-used from another building and indeed they appeared to have been made specifically for the present structure.

A possible explanation of this unusual occurrence is that posts were prepared but set on one side until further preparation and erection of the frame was undertaken. The third Earl of Southampton inherited his title and estates as a young boy in 1581. It is possible that he, or his advisers, set about planning a new barn at Posbrook but that construction was held up in the 1590s when he got into serious financial and political difficulties. These difficulties were resolved early in the reign of James 1 and the Earl would then have been in a position to order the completion of the work.

The Market Hall and St. Margaret's Priory

Titchfield market hall, now splendidly restored and re-erected at The Weald

and Downland Open Air Museum at Singleton, was generally thought to have been the creation of the third Earl of Southampton and this assumption has been confirmed by a tree-ring date of 1619.

More unexpected was the date of 1623 established for St. Margaret's Priory. St. Margaret's was by some supposed to have been an Elizabethan house, partly because it appears on the estate map of 1605-10. However, the image on the map appears as a typical Elizabethan E-plan house, whereas St. Margaret's is a long house under a single ridge with a tower at one gable end. Inside is a very fine Jacobean staircase leading up to a suite of two splendid rooms both with a beautiful painted frieze below a high, coved ceiling. The quality of these rooms is far above what would be expected of country gentlemen of the time and it has led experts to surmise that this was a house in which the third Earl intended to entertain fellow courtiers, or even the king. It has also been suggested that the brick tower was built to allow the king and his attendants to climb to a viewing platform at the top in order to watch hunting in the Earl's deer park.

These suggestions are attractive but not without their problems. The tower certainly has stairs rising to a viewing platform at the top but these stairs are narrow and cramped and hardly suited to royal or aristocratic guests. Furthermore, records show that Arthur Bromfield, a gentleman and the Earl's agent was living at St. Margaret's with his family after the present house was built in 1623. This, however, need not be such a problem. The house of 1623, which lacked a kitchen, was certainly not a family house. It was rather a

house for entertaining aristocrats for short periods. It is highly likely that the Elizabethan house would have been retained for Bromfield and his family who could keep an eye on the grand house of 1623 and arrange for it to be made ready for aristocratic use.

Of course, there is much that can only be a matter of informed debate but, with scientifically established dates of construction for some of Titchfield's more important buildings, this debate can be more focused and believable.

Edward Roberts

THE TITCHFIELD BEACON

There was, once, a Beacon in the Parish of Titchfield. The position on the 1605/10 map called 'The Beacons' (see Fig.1.) is in the area now known as Park Gate. Also shown, to the north of 'The Beacons' is 'Swanwyck Gatte', where the road from 'Swannycke Heath' enters the fenced region shown as 'Swannick'. From the 'contours' (indications of hills and adjoining slopes) of the map 'The Beacons' is located on a hill, which appears to be the highest at that place.

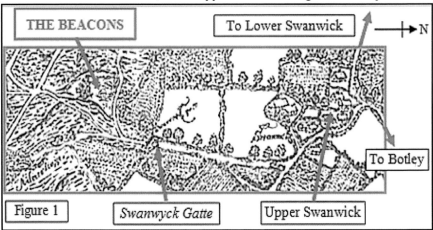

Figure 1

Referring to the 1810 and 1841 Ordnance Survey maps (see Fig. 2), a beacon called 'Bushy Beacon' is indicated to the west of the road from Park Gate to

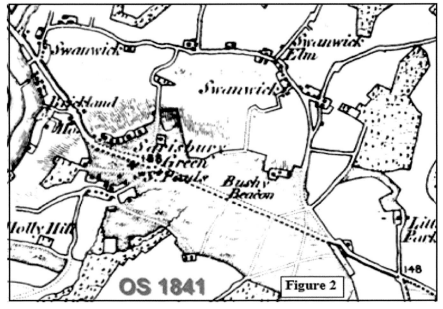

Figure 2

46

Upper Swanwick and Botley, and there is reasonable correlation between the positions on the 1610 map and the Ordnance Survey maps.

Position of the Titchfield Beacon - the highest point

Investigation of the actual site indicates that the area to the west of the Botley Road (at the northern end of Park Gate) is, at 56 metres, just higher than its surroundings. It is now a housing estate and the roads within the estate are dominated by the word 'Beacon'. i.e. Beacon Mount, Beacon Way, Beacon Close and, at the lowest part, Beacon Bottom - Beacon Mount has a slope rather greater than is normal for the district. Fig. 3 shows the layout of the roads surrounding the Titchfield Beacon site. The current topography indicates that the representation on the 1605/10 map was largely correct.

Speed's map of 1611 shows a beacon in the same area, as do maps by Blaeu of the same period. There are, also, other references of the Titchfield Beacon and to a beacon at Sarisbury which is, clearly, the same beacon. Other references to a beacon at Bitterne, and one in West End, can be found, and there are constant references of beacons on Portsdown Hill, Butser Hill and the Isle of Wight. The beacon system has been in existence from at least medieval times and the beacon at Park Gate would seem to be part of that system, as it is unlikely that it would have been introduced simply for maritime reasons during the 'Armada Panic'. It would have been used for communication purposes danger warnings, celebrations and news - and it is obvious, from visual investigation, that the view from the top would have been spectacular, with Portsdown Hill, Butser Hill, the Isle of Wight, Calshot, Bitterne and the downs to the north, from Winchester to Petersfield, clearly seen.

The 1605/10 map indicates that most of the adjacent area was heath land with few, or no, trees, but now the surrounding landscape is covered in buildings and substantial trees which, sadly, obstruct the views.

Ken Groves.

MARGARET OF ANJOU 1430-1482

One of the first places that Margaret of Anjou, niece of Charles VII of France, visited when she first came to England, in 1445 to marry King Henry VI, was the parish of Titchfield. The wedding was held in Titchfield Abbey on April 23rd, with Cardinal Beaufort in attendance, together with the majority of the dignitaries in the country.

A Royal Marraige

She landed, from France, within Portsmouth Harbour, probably at Portchester. She spent her first night at Southwick Priory, travelling to Titchfield for the wedding on the next day, crossing Stoney Bridge to reach the Abbey; hence the habit of mis-calling the bridge Anjou Bridge. It quickly became obvious that the man she married suffered from mental problems, and Margaret took an ever-increasing part in helping to run the country. There is evidence that she did nothing to improve the muddled finances of the King and this, together with her abrasive manner, and moralistic attitude, resulted in a lack of approval by the English. She is blamed for the final loss of most of the land in France, which Henry V had conquered, but this did herald the end of the Hundred Years War during 1453/4. Margaret had only one child, Edward of Westminster born in October 1453, and it was her determination to ensure that he was to become the next King of England which instigated the War of the Roses; both parties, the Lancastrians and the Yorkists appear to have had equal rights to claim the throne.

After numerous battles, with both sides achieving victories, Margaret was finally defeated at the Battle of Tewkesbury in 1471, when her son was killed, becoming the only Prince of Wales to die in battle. Together with King Henry, she was imprisoned in the Tower, and Henry was killed, leaving Edward IV as King. Margaret was sent back to France, temporarily broken in spirit, but she survived, having recovered her acerbity and ruthlessness, until the age of 52, dying in 1482.

Ken Groves

THE LAST PLANTAGENET

Few local people are aware that the last member of the Plantagenet dynasty was born in the Meon Valley and for some years lived beside the river in Segensworth manor house.

Arthur Plantagenet, later Viscount Lisle, was the illegitimate son of Edward IV: the Princes in the Tower were his legitimate brothers. Arthur's mother Elizabeth was a daughter of a family of wealthy Hampshire woollen merchants, the Waytes, who held a number of Hampshire properties including the now vanished fulling mill at Little Fontley. His father Edward, a Yorkist, had seized the throne in a rebellion of 1461.

Edward was an attractive and athletic young man, and had probably met Elizabeth during a royal progress in southern England. Arthur seems to have been born at the Wayte family home in Soberton in 1462. Edward briefly lost the throne in 1470, but returned in 1471 to bring the Lancastrian line to an end, and to reign until 1483. He had married Elizabeth Woodville in 1464; she bore him four children, Edward and Richard (the ill-fated Princes in the Tower), and Elizabeth and Catherine, all of them younger half brothers and sisters of Arthur. Arthur was not forgotten.

When he was ten his father paid for a suit of clothes that the tailor described as 'for my lord the Bastard'. But as the fate of Edward and Richard was to show, in the feverish atmosphere of the Wars of the Roses, it was very dangerous to possess any of 'the blood royal', whether legitimately or illegitimately. So Arthur's Wayte family chose to keep their grandson out of the public eye.

Arthur grew up in comfortable obscurity at Soberton, living the life of an undistinguished country gentleman. Against the odds, he managed to survive the blood letting of Richard III's reign, and of the early years of Henry VII.

Henry was the first of the Tudors, a family with an even sketchier claim to the 'blood royal' than Arthur himself. So Arthur kept himself at Soberton throughout his twenties and thirties. But Henry had proudly married Arthur's half sister Elizabeth, bringing the red and white roses together, and as she too grew up she began to take an interest in her older brother. In 1502, when he was 40, she took him into her household, where he was known as Master Arthur.

Arthur wisely made no attempt to take advantage of his privileged position. It was not until Henry VII's death in 1509, and the succession of the self-confident young king Henry VIII that Arthur's career began to flourish. Henry, his nephew, was quite happy at this stage to recognise his middle-aged uncle, calling him 'Cos'.

In 1511 Arthur married his first wife, Elizabeth Grey, Lady Lisle, from whom he was to take his title. She was a widow with three sons, and with Arthur had three daughters, Frances, Elizabeth and Bridget. It was probably at this time that he moved from the family home at Soberton to another Wayte property, Segensworth in Titchfield parish. He was now Sheriff of Hampshire, Warden of the Forest of Bere and Vice-Admiral of the Kingdom; a post which made it necessary to be near Portchester and Portsmouth. In 1514 he took an active part in the defence of the south coast against French raids. The overall commander, the Earl of Surrey, put him in charge of operations: 'methink Master Arthur to be the most convenient considering that the country regards him as the best of any man hereabouts'. At the same time, Arthur was now an energetic business man, keeping a ship called the Mary Plantagenet at Southampton, and several ships at Fareham.

Arthur's first wife Elizabeth died in 1523; she was buried in the church of Titchfield Abbey, just across the road from Segensworth manor house. Five years later, now aged 66, he married another wealthy widow, Honor Grenville, acquiring eight more stepchildren, five boys and three girls. He still had no male heir of his own.

Tudor politics were now entering a dark period. Arthur's nephew, the king, was in the process of divorcing his wife Katherine, and breaking with the Papacy. All the nobility were anticipating that the monasteries would be dissolved. Arthur was hoping to acquire Titchfield Abbey, but he was thwarted by a young and ruthless rival, Thomas Wriothesley. In 1533, aged 71, Arthur was appointed royal Viceroy in Calais, England's last foothold in Europe, possibly to get him out of this country during the momentous events here. Arthur and Honor left Segensworth for the last time. They were to enjoy seven years in Calais: but in the murky political atmosphere, they were not safe even there.

In 1540, on the orders of the king's tyrannical minister Thomas Cromwell, Arthur was summoned to London, arrested on suspicion of treason, and committed to the Tower. It was thought by the public that he would be executed. He may have been spared partly because one of his stepdaughters, Anne Grenville, was one of the young women around the court who caught Henry's eye: perhaps Henry thought it best not to execute a possible future father-in-law (fortunately for Anne nothing came of it). More important, the king fell out with Thomas Cromwell, who was himself executed. Someone now reminded the king that his uncle was in the Tower, and Henry sent his own signet to Arthur with a message that he was to be released. Sadly, Arthur was unable to cope with the shock, and died without leaving the Tower. He was 80.

None of Arthur's family ever returned to Segensworth. A final melancholy footnote to the story is that when Wriothesley was converting the abbey into Place House, Arthur had written asking that the remains of his first wife Elizabeth should be moved to Titchfield parish church. We do not know whether this was ever done.

George Watts

The Lisle Letters, ed. Muriel St. Clair Byrne, 1983

BEE BOLES AT PLACE HOUSE

Many visitors to the ruins of Place House fail to notice the four bricked-up alcoves located east of the Chapter House site in the south face of the northern boundary wall. These are bee boles - wall recesses in which straw beehives or skeps were kept in the days before the general introduction of sugar replaced honey as a common sweetener. The use of bee boles was wide-spread through-

Place House wall showing the bee boles

out the country, remains being found not only in the gardens of great houses but in outbuildings of small cottages and farms. The local building material was used, usually brick or stone; wooden remains vanished long ago.

Size was determined by the material, brick wall bee boles tending to be smaller because the brick walls were usually thinner than those of stone. The recess was usually between 18 and 30 inches high, 14 and 21 inches across, running about 18 inches into the wall. In this way the hives were protected from rain and wind while still being easily accessible to the bees. Those at Place House are of two sizes. The two upper boles are 29 inches across the opening and 15 inches to the crown, while the lower pair are 25 inches wide and rise to 17 inches.

"Rain and weather eat your hives. .and cold most of all is hurtful for your Bees. you must have an house made along a sure dry wall in your Garden near or in your Orchard. For Bees love flowers and wood with all their hearts."

The usual position for bee boles was not too near any noisy or busy place. They do not often face onto a pathway or road where passing traffic and people might disturb them "...for Bees love not to be molested. . . Bees of all creatures love cleanliness and peace". However apiarists in the 17th and 18th centuries were advised that .."Bees habituated to the sight of the family will become less ferocious and more tractable" and in some cases bee boles are found in the outside walls of houses or even over the door. As at Place House they usually face south where they are warmed by the sun enabling early and late working for the bees who may thus be wide awake.."for cold begets sloth."

Written evidence of bee keeping is found from Anglo-Saxon and Norman times. In medieval England, indeed until the introduction of sugar as a sweetener, bee keeping was essential to the national economy. Honey was often used to pay rents; 'honey tithes' were quite common. It is recorded that King Edward I bought a cask of honey at the Honey Fair held in Conway; this fair was still well known in the 19th century.

The wax produced from the bees' glands to construct honeycomb was in the past often considered to be more important than the honey itself. Beeswax candles burn cleaner than tallow or rush lights and were always used as altar candles in the Pre - Reformation Church, for as the Gwentian Code said: "The origin of bees is from Paradise and because of the sin of man they came thence; and God conferred His grace upon them, and therefore the mass cannot be sung without the wax". The uses of beeswax were many. Tough stitching that had to last was made with waxed thread, so it was used by cobblers, tailors, sailmakers, ropemakers, leatherworkers, saddlers and harnessmakers. It has been used to provide a watertight seal for containers from Greek amphorae to the soil sampling tubes of today's civil engineers. It has long been recognised as the prime ingredient of good polish because it is easily soluble in turpentine. In modern times it is used in the treatment of arthritis, the manufacture of cosmetics and it forms the base of zinc-and-castor oil.

The use of honey in medical preparations was recognised from early times, particularly if mixed with herbs. For example, a brew of honey and garlic was used to treat asthma, bronchitis, whooping cough and tuberculosis, while the Romans concocted oxmel from lettuce soaked in vinegar and honey for treatment of insomnia, constipation, poor lactation and pain relief. In our own lives, we are all familar with the comfort of honey and lemon to sooth a sore throat!

Wise gardeners have always attracted bees as pollinating agents by providing such plants as lavender and rosemary among many others for, as Thomas More commented. . . "my bees love them".

From ancient times the fermentation of honey and water into mead has been practised worldwide and indeed the name varies little from 'rneth' in German, 'methu' in Greek, 'madhu' in Indian and 'medus' in Lithuanian. The Bible mentions honey in many contexts but perhaps Solomon summed it up best: "My son, eat thou honey, because it is good.

Of local interest is the fact that the bodies of the 3rd Earl of Southampton and his eldest son may still remain, apparently uncorrupted, in lead coffins full of honey in the vault at St Peter's Church!

Sources:
Discovering Bee Keeping by Daphne More
Honey by Isha Mellor

Annie Mitchell

54

CHILLING AND THE DUDLEY CONSPIRICY

England 1556. A blazing comet was seen in the sky for several weeks, watched with fear and misgivings by many. Comets were widely considered to herald major upheaval or great change. Within a short time court officials became aware that a dangerous conspiracy was hatching that threatened the very monarchy. The plotters' motive was fear that England's Catholic Queen Mary Tudor was planning to have her Spanish husband Philip crowned as king, thus threatening with persecution the English Protestant subjects.

This was the latest in a series of three conspiracies against Queen Mary. One of the chief instigators was Henry Sutton Dudley, a close associate of his second cousin Robert Dudley, later Queen Elizabeth's Earl of Leicester. In July 1553 he had been implicated in the political manœuvres of his kinsman John Dudley, the Duke of Northumberland, to place his daughter-in-law, Protestant Lady Jane Grey on the throne in place of the rightful heir, Catholic Mary, daughter of Henry VIII. When this failed, Northumberland was executed and Henry Dudley was imprisoned in the Tower of London but was pardoned by Queen Mary (above) in October 1553.

In 1554 there was another failed rebellion, with Lady Jane Grey as the unwitting figurehead, led by Thomas Wyatt, which resulted in their executions.

After the marriage of Queen Mary to Philip of Spain, discontent and unrest continued. Henry Dudley and other dissatisfied citizens laid plans for a plot which comprised those in embittered opposition to the government together with military and royal officers who had not been paid or had even been discharged. Disaffection was rife even among Catholics. All hoped for some personal profit from a successful rebellion.

His fellow conspirators were John Throckmorton and his kinsman Nicholas. Other participants were Sir Anthony Kingston who was a keen supporter of Edward Courtney, Earl of Devon, Christopher Ashton, John Bedell and Richard Uvedale, Captain of Yarmouth Castle, whose home was at Chilling near Titchfield. Encouragement was offered by the French Ambassador, Antoine de Noailles, without the full approval of his government and monarch.

Henry Dudley was once Captain of the Guard at Boulogne and had many friends in France. He had been well received by King Henry II of France but returned home with only a vague promise of assistance in the endeavour.

Henry Dudley and his accomplices moved in January 1556 to conceal stores of ammunition in several locations and also secured £50,000 from the Exchequer where Dudley had a number of friends. At the time of the appearance of the comet, this move was made against the Treasury. To heighten the alarm and despondency among the London residents, diversionary fires were started in different parts of the city.

On 2nd February, Dudley and Throckmorton arrived at Richard Uvedale's house at Chilling; very conveniently placed with access to the coast in a quiet area not overlooked or guarded. Uvedale was led to believe that Dudley wished to leave England for France as he was in debt. Uvedale was prepared to help and sent across to Yarmouth Castle, on the Isle of Wight, for a boat. While they waited for a few days until the boat was organised, Uvedale learned that Dudley was also planning to approach dissidents living in exile in France to organise an army to be landed at Portsmouth to assist in the overthrow of Queen Mary and her Spanish supporters.

By 10th March, Henry Dudley was again at Chilling and Richard Uvedale provided a boat to France. The next time he returned, Dudley planned to arrive with the armed support from France. Uvedale was able to confirm that there would be no resistance in the Isle of Wight and so, Dudley left for France to make final preparations. Richard Uvedale, as Captain of Yarmouth Castle, was to ensure that a safe harbour was prepared for the returning exiles, mercenaries and hidden money from the Exchequer.

Sir Anthony Kingston, a Gloucestershire man who had already shown violent opposition to Queen Mary's Bill recalling Catholic exiles early in 1555, was set to raise 6,000 men in the West Country and approach London in support of Edward Courtney who, it was hoped, would marry Princess Elizabeth and she would supplant Mary as Queen.

Great Chilling: Warsash

Anne Dale

The difficulty faced by the conspirators was in co-ordinating their efforts while maintaining security; the size, geographical spread and diversity of the plot made it difficult and unmanageable. The passage of time and inevitable indiscretions by individuals led to the plot coming to the notice of the government who then moved swiftly and arrested the troublemakers. It was at this point that Cardinal Pole learned of the attempt on the Treasury through evidence provided by Thomas White, one of the officials. Among those arrested were John Bedell, Richard Uvedale and John Throckmorton. Sir William Kingston was also arrested but died on the way to London. Had the French Ambassador not fled, he too would have been taken into custody. Edward Courtney left for Italy where he died of pneumonia. It all came to nothing. Most of them were imprisoned in the Tower and would endure examination, torture and trial; all were executed. Henry Dudley was still in France and so escaped arrest and punishment. He became an exile in the French service from 1556 to 1563 and then returned to England, where he died sometime between 1568 and 1570.

So ended the episode which saw Chilling involved in national events. Chilling Manor was the home some 50 years later of Henry Timberlake who is the subject of another chapter of this book. Chilling Manor Farm is now a riding centre. The seriously dilapidated old house had survived until 1951 when it was demolished. In the 1980s the present house was built on the same site, its dimensions exactly matching the ground plan of the original.

1. *Calendar of State Papers Domestic 1556.*
2. *Mary Tudor – The Spanish Tudor* by H. F. M. Prescott.
3. *Two Tudor Conspiracies* by David Loades.

Annie Mitchell

Place House, Titchfield

AN EARLY 17TH CENTURY MAP OF TITCHFIELD

The tradition of creating estate maps of English properties begins in the early 1570s, with more appearing in the 1580s. Local maps had been prepared for other purposes, primarily military and legal, exceptionally in the late medieval period, and more commonly during the sixteenth century.[1] Christopher Saxton surveyed the country for his well-known series of county maps, engraved and printed between 1574 and 1579, and the work was subsequently assembled into a wall map of the whole country, published in 1583.[2]

Fig 1 - Early 17th Century Map

Many landowners must first have seen images of their locality in Saxton's series, and these printed maps may well have been the inspiration for at least some private landowners to document their holdings, commissioning fine images of their estates that might be displayed, much as Henry VIII had framed maps of his kingdom for the walls of his palaces.[3]

The last two decades of the sixteenth century and the first three of the seventeenth saw the production of many fine estate maps, with elaborate decoration, colour and imagery, creating a powerful vision of the late Elizabethan and early Stuart countryside. For all, they might be a calculated step in land management, documenting property and rights. These maps appear across England - but estate mapping depended on private initiative, and many of them were not intended for display, that is, the information they contained

Fig 2

was not shared, and might be kept private, especially for legal reasons. Institutional owners seem to have been more cautious about displaying the results of surveys: maps with institutional rather than private origins are more modest in terms of ornamentation and decoration. Indeed, it has only been with the development of local authority record offices and the description of private estate archives that it has been possible to see the patterns of overall development in mapping, and the results show interesting contrasts.[4] Before 1700, Hampshire was less well mapped than many parts of the country: a rough calculation suggests that there may have been about 16 maps per 1000 square miles: Buckinghamshire had 125, Essex 115 and Sussex 84.[5] The main factor in this difference appears to have been the reluctance of some institutional landlords - and much land in Hampshire was in the hands of ecclesiastical and collegiate bodies - to have their properties mapped. The map of Titchfield and the surrounding area therefore represents a particularly valuable component in our knowledge of the Hampshire countryside at the start of the seventeenth century.

The map formed part of the muniments of the Earls of Southampton, which passed to the Delmé family around 1775. Despite attempts to trace it, there has been no published reference based directly on the original since around 1906, when it was described by the Reverend G.W.Minns in the *Proceedings of the Hampshire Field Club*, and a lithograph redrawing of the map by Mr

Wilberforce Cobbett was published at the same time. This article is our prime source of information for the map.[6] One small section of it, covering Place House (that is, the Earl of Southampton's mansion, the former Premonstratensian abbey), was reproduced as a line drawing in the third volume of the *Victoria County History* for Hampshire, taken directly from the image that appeared in an earlier article by Minns, on Titchfield Abbey and Place House, also written for the Hampshire Field Club.

In the Titchfield Miscellanea at Hampshire Record Office is what appears to be a full-size tracing of the area around Place House (94M84/70), which is exactly coterminous with the excerpt printed in the Victoria County History.[7] Minns tells us that the map was on several sheets of parchment (probably four, just possibly three, or five or more), with an overall measurement of 6' 9" by 4' 8". That the map was drawn out on several sheets in this way also suggests that the intention was to view it as a whole, and that it may well have been intended for display. Some maps prepared for institutions were broken down into sections, or were drawn so that they did not fill more than a single membrane - often of uniform size and shape, much as if they were sheets of a printed atlas.

The linear scale at which Wilberforce Cobbett's reproduction was printed was about a quarter of the original, which must have been close to a foot to one mile. The reproduction in the *VCH* is proportionately larger, at about three-quarters of the original size, and it is especially useful for giving us more information than can be seen on the reproduction of the whole map. It is possible that the *VCH* section is also based on Wilberforce Cobbett's redrawing: it contains a few words, particularly the smaller of the two legends 'dogg kennell', which, while present on Minns' reproduction, are no more than a blur and cannot be made distinct. This is important because it suggests that Cobbett's redrawing was in fact more detailed than we can now see from the reduced reproduction: there are several places where there are legends that were not picked out by Minns for numbering and comment, and there may be other areas where what are now simply indistinct blurs were once further legends. Examples of these may be on the foreshore along the banks of the Meon. There may be traces of further captions which have not reproduced well enough to transcribe, for example, going north from Hook, and below the 'sea fence'.

The map covers an extensive area, approximately 18.5 km². It is bounded by the River Hamble at the west and north, although it includes part of Bursledon on the west bank. At the south-eastern edge, it runs from east of Tichfield Haven north along the River Meon nearly as far as Shedfield. The area is both less and more than the parish of Titchfield. Minns' statement that it is not a map of the Wriothesley family estate, as it includes Hook, which was a separate manor, is erroneous: the evidence is overwhelmingly that this is exactly what the document was, a map of the Wriothesley estates. Hook had passed to Thomas Wriothesley, first Earl of Southampton, by 1550, in a series of property transactions through which the Earl bought lands beyond those formerly owned by Titchfield Abbey. Wriothesley had for example a holding in Bursledon, which is presumably the part of that village also covered by the map.[8] Work to assemble the estate had even anticipated the Dissolution: interests in the manor of Brownwich (or Brownwich Chilling) and Meon were acquired from the Uvedale family in 1536 and in April 1538, from Sir Thomas Wyatt.[9] Some parts of Titchfield parish, particularly to the north-east, are given by the map in only the barest outline, and it is likely that these areas were not owned by the Earl of Southampton.

The map was made probably around 1605. The dating cannot be precise, but a number of indications points to this. It must have been drawn before 1611, when the marsh between Titchfield and the Haven was enclosed by a sea wall. It also dates from before the making of the supposed canal that went with it.[10] The map has no cartouche setting out for whom it was made, or the name of a surveyor, or a date. It does, however, include the statement 'This copps felled in Anno D. 1605' in a space that was left blank to take this caption. The most likely explanation for this retrospective comment is that this was a change that took place between the surveying work and the engrossment of the map. We know from the records of contemporary map-makers that surveying was a seasonal activity, and that some time, in some instances up to two years, might elapse between the taking of the survey in the field - for which in some rare instances we have drafts, showing triangulation and sketches of field shapes, and of buildings - and the engrossment of the map on parchment.[11] The handwriting on the map is consistent with a late sixteenth- or early seventeenth-century date.

If the Wriothesley Earls of Southampton derived their Titchfield estate substantially from the lands of Titchfield Abbey, they had other property in Hampshire drawn from former monastic possessions, including those of Beaulieu Abbey, Quarr Abbey and Hyde Abbey, as well as property that had belonged to St Elizabeth's College, Winchester. Among these were estates at Stratton, Micheldever, and North Stoneham (this last was sold to the Fleming family in 1599). There are no other estate maps of their property in this area, however, that are contemporary with the Titchfield map, and those that survive for these properties, like the earliest estate map of Stratton, date from the eighteenth century.[12]

A detailed examination of the Titchfield map provides us with some important information about the topography of the area and allows us to set it in the context of contemporary estate maps. The reproduction has west at the top, and almost certainly this was the way in which the map was originally oriented. Buildings are drawn as if viewed obliquely from the east. It was not uncommon for maps of this period to be oriented as best suited the lie of the estate. A map of Hursley and the surrounding area prepared around 1588 is similarly oriented, with west at the top.[13] There is comparatively little decoration on the map: the compass rose, images of huntsmen, deer at several points, and ships along the Hamble, at Titchfield Haven, and on the Meon, at Warebridge ('Vermans Bridge' on the map), along with symbolic depictions of woodland and of elevated terrain. The map as we have it now has no overall border. It gives us a fine overall picture of a landscape, with much heathland, woodland, parks and small enclosed fields, divided between arable and fallow. There is little trace at this point of the open fields of Titchfield. There is equally little on the map that links directly to the management of the land: it has no indication of ownership attached to properties, and the captions do not relate directly to questions of estate activity, aside from the dated reference to the felling of the copse. It is possible that the original map contained some information of this nature, either expressed in words (perhaps less likely given that so much was transcribed by Wilberforce Cobbett), or by the use of colour.

Many of the places are identified in captions. These appear to have been written in a single hand, at an angle that rises slightly from start to finish. Some of the placenames, such as Swanwick Heath and Fareham Heath, were written in spaces that had been left blank on the map; a few, such as Fareham Parke, were written throughout in capital letters but in the same hand. It is just possible that a second hand may have annotated the map, or written a second set of captions. The image in the *VCH* of The Place includes the dog kennel, which is captioned twice, and the caption set within the kennel itself may be in another hand. Beyond farm and field names, features identified include 'The cornar of fox' and 'The beacon', both on Swannick Heath; two deer leaps on Swannick Heath, and the 'Great beeche' to the north west of The Place. The reproduction of the whole map by Minns provides a key to many of the place names. There are a few further in addition, for example, to the south of Talboots Wode (62 on Minns' map) is a building without chimneys, probably identified by the word 'barne'; immediately to the east of Southe feilde (58) is 'Whittleacre cloos'; to the south of 67, Crafton Churche, 'Crafton' is written in the street; and to east of 72, the caption 'Hooke house' is repeated. There are also a few mistranscriptions on the Minns' key: for example, Crabthorne (60), reads 'Crabhorne'.

St Margaret's Farm (Rev. Minns)

Scattered across the map are representations of buildings, from small houses to the much larger establishments at The Place and Whitle Howse, and churches. The depiction of these buildings contains considerable stylised detail. Although some contemporary maps made distinctions which might reflect the buildings themselves, for example, showing roofing materials such as thatch and tile, the evidence that they are more than schematic representations is ambiguous. Maps were often drawn up at a distance both of time and physical space from the locality surveyed. A surveyor had the notes he took in the field, but we know that in the preparation of the final map features might vary: we have examples of draft maps, for instance, which show perspective views of houses from one side, and the engrossment shows them from the opposite side.[14] In this way, there is nothing inherently surprising about the depiction of the houses in the town of Titchfield where it is difficult to establish exactly how the buildings are aligned: some may be drawn at right-angles to the roads, rather than parallel with them (Fig 2). The surveyor will have made up his engrossment following the spirit of his notes, providing an image of town and country, rather than an exact representation. At the same time the map gives a good general indication of the layout of the town, the houses with their backyards or closes, with the church at the eastern edge. The depiction of arable also needs careful interpretation: directions of ploughing are shown, and a very few fields, for example, to the immediate south of Titchfield itself, show fields with the ploughing in more than one direction, perhaps representing some earlier division in terms of ownership, or a practical solution to field management and drainage. No impression is given in the depiction of the town of Titchfield of the rise and fall of the topography. Relief is shown in some places, particularly on the heaths, with hills indicated by 'humps', much like the contemporary drawings of this sort of terrain on Saxton's county maps. Like many maps of the period, there is a schematic use of trees in field boundaries, and they also appear in clumps to represent woodland. The detail of the *VCH* image also allows us to see that some, at least, of the field boundaries were in fact wooden pales, perhaps unsurprisingly for parks. The ships on the map may indicate the extent to which the rivers were navigable: the Hamble has a vessel quite some way beyond the village of Bursledon, just at the bend before the caption 'Botly Rivar'.

Colour may have added much to the finished product. Minns noted that the map appeared to have been tinted, and that slight traces remained; he believed that damp conditions had been responsible for the loss of this. We can see parallels in the effect of display on pigments in, for example, the leaching out of colour on a map of Southampton and the immediate area that is probably of late sixteenth-century date.[15] Wilberforce Cobbett's redrawing shows two levels of stippling for the foreshore, which may give some idea of tidal reach and which may well have been represented in colour.

It is very difficult to adduce any evidence about the way in which the map was prepared and what sort of surveying instruments may have been used. It is possible that high points were used for triangulation: the map has a reasonable level of cadastral accuracy. Other surveyors made use of church towers and hill tops for this purpose, both of which appear on this map.

Although the original of the Titchfield map has disappeared, and may not survive, there can be little doubt of its authenticity. The original must have been a wholly typical example of the work of the land surveyors of the late sixteenth and early seventeenth centuries, and Wilberforce Cobbett's redrawing of it is an accomplished piece of work. We can only lament the disappearance of such an important and impressive map.

C.M.Woolgar

References.
1.*Local maps and plans from medieval England* ed. R.A.Skelton and P.D.A.Harvey (Oxford, 1986); for local examples, especially military maps, Maps of Portsmouth before 1801: a catalogue ed. D.Hodson (Portsmouth Record Series 4; 1978); P.D.A.Harvey, 'English estate maps: their early history and their use as historical evidence', in Rural images: estate maps in the old and new worlds ed. D.Buisseret (Chicago, 1996), pp. 27-61, at pp. 27-30.

2.Discussed in S.Tyacke and J.Huddy Christopher *Saxton and Tudor mapmaking*

3.As well as foreign cities and depictions of sieges: *The inventory of King Henry VIII*, Society of Antiquaries MS 129 and British Library MS Harley 1419 ed. D.Starkey (3vols., London, 1999-)

4.A.S.Bendall Maps, land and society: a history, with a carto-bibliography of Cambridgeshire estate maps, c.1600-1836 (Cambridge, 1992) summarises developments in estate mapping after extensive work to assemble a corpus of maps of Cambridgeshire.

*5.*Bendall Maps, land and society, p. 3; Harvey, *'English estate maps: their early history'*,

*6.*G.W.Minns, 'Remarks on an old map of a portion of the ancient parish of Titchfield', Papers and proceedings of the Hampshire Field Club and Archaeological Society, 5. (1904-6) pp. 203-9; K.Hayward, 'In search of the Titchfield map', Hampshire Field Club Newsletter, new series, 8 (Autumn 1987) pp. 4-5. The map was also shown to a party from the Hampshire Field club by Wilberforce Cobbett: Hampshire Chronicle, 13 May 1899. I am grateful to George Watts and Keith Hayward for this information. The map is available on-line at www.geog.port.ac.uk/webmap/hantscat/html/h0107429.htm accessed 10 June 2009.

*7.*G.W.Minns, *'Titchfield Abbey and Place House'*, Papers and proceedings of the Hampshire Field Club and Archaeological Society, 3 (1894-7) pp. 317-38; VCH Hampshire, iii, pp. 220-33, at p. 220. There is no mention of the map in the editorial notes for the Titchfield section of the Hampshire VCH: University of Southampton Library, MS 29/68. HRO 94M84/70. I owe the Titchfield Miscellanea reference to Keith Hayward.

*8.*Hampshire Record Office 5M53/115, sale of Hook Valence, 15 December 1547; 5M53/117, sale of East Hook, 27 May 1549; and a further transaction, 5M53/541, covering the interests of the Earl of Salisbury in Hook Mortimer, 16 November 1611. VCH Hampshire, iii, pp. 283-4.

*9.*The National Archives, E40/A3235, summarised in A descriptive catalogue of the ancient deeds in the Public Record Office ed. H.C.Maxwell Lyte (5 vols., London, 1890-1906) ii, p. 169.

10.Titchfield: a history ed. D.G.Watts (Titchfield, 1982) p. 57.

*11.*C.M.Woolgar, *'Some draft estate maps of the early seventeenth century'*, Cartographic Journal, 22 (1985) pp. 136-43.

*12.*Hampshire Record Office 92M95/F8/5/1.

13.Reproduced in The medieval park: new perspectives ed. R.Liddiard (Macclesfield, 2007)

*14.*Woolgar, *'Some draft estate maps'*, p. 140, pages 5 and 6, Lower Heyford village.

*15.*University of Southampton Library MS 2/2, reproduced for the Southampton Record Series in 1964, accompanied by E.Welch Southampton maps from Elisabethan times: an introduction to 24 facsimiles (Southampton Record Series, 9; 1964) pp. 1-2

Fig 1. Place House, Titchfield from the Victoria County History.

Fig 2. Titchfield and fields to the south as far as Posbrook Farm, with the River Meon and Warebridge on the eastern side showing in red, the numbers added by Minns to his Hampshire Field Club Publication.

Reproduced from Wilberforce Cobbett's redrawing.

THE MEON ESTUARY

The closure of the tidal estuary of the River Meon is one of the most significant incidents in the history of Titchfield Parish: the village ceased to be a small port at the head of a navigable tidal channel. Yet surprisingly little reliable historical evidence survives of the event and its aftermath. Instead, stories of all kinds have circulated in the village for over two hundred years: it was built by Dutchmen; because he was responsible, an effigy of the third Earl of Southampton was burned at the annual bonfire day; King Charles I had hidden under Hammonds Bridge in 1648; there had once been windlasses for mooring vessels below the parish church; and so on. The account the History Society gave in *Titchfield: A History* 1982 was based largely on such village traditions. But in recent years members of the Society have worked hard - and argued furiously - to establish a more accurate account of what happened, and much has emerged. Contributions of four of them follow. Readers are invited to examine them critically, and come to their own conclusions.

George Watts

67

THE TITCHFIELD CANAL - A MATTER OF INTERPRETATION?

Introduction

There is a man-made watercourse to the west of the River Meon in Hampshire, known generally today as The Titchfield Canal, which links the village of Titchfield to the northern shore of the Solent. Many publications, websites and even Fareham Borough Council documents claim that it "...is one of the oldest canals in the country..."(1) and reiterate the local tradition that it was constructed around 1611 for the 3rd Earl of Southampton. There is a further local tradition that a Dutch engineer was brought in to carry out the work. The canal was deemed to have been a failure and was later used to feed water meadows. Until recently, despite decades of research by local historians, no solid information has come to light regarding the construction of this feature and adherents to the traditional story can only invoke assumption, coincidence, conjecture and imagination to support their views.

The absence of an Act of Parliament has been used to support the arguments of both proponents and opponents of this traditional view. This is totally irrelevant. These Acts were required in cases of linear transportation links such as canals, roads and railways to establish wayleave; the right of access across the properties of a number of landowners. In the case under consideration the whole of the watercourse was located within land owned by one person and hence, any such Act would be unnecessary.

There are several documents in existence which are of interest in relation to this matter but they are, based upon the currently accepted interpretation, mutually incompatible and do not support the locally held traditional views. They are the Titchfield Parish Register for 1589 - 1634 (2), the Indenture of 1620 setting up the original Earl of Southampton's Trust (3) and the transcript of the subsequent court case of 1742, Attorney General v William Churcher (4). The incompatibility may be removed by a reinterpretation of the meaning of the remark in the Parish Register. This, together with later archival evidence leads to the conclusion that the watercourse may well have been constructed over half a century later and for a different purpose than traditionally supposed.

The Parish Register

The comment in the Titchfield Parish Register for the 24 June 1611 that "the same day Titchfield Haven was shut out by one Richard Talbotts industrie under gods permisione at the costs of the right honourable the Earle of Southampton" is the one piece of evidence which underpins the whole of the story. This comment has always been taken to mean that the mouth of the estuary of the River was shut off from the sea as regards navigation by coastal trading vessels. An assumption followed that the watercourse to the west of the River must have been a canal constructed by the 3rd Earl of Southampton at about the same time in order to maintain a waterborne transport link between Titchfield and the Solent. This is not borne out by the contents of the Indenture of 1620 and is totally contradictory to the contents of the transcript of the court case of 1742, both of which will be examined in due course. An alternative interpretation can be made which does accord with these later sources.

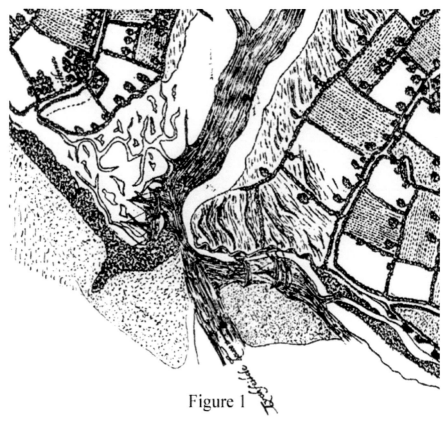

Figure 1

The Parish Register comment stating that "... Titchfield Haven was shutt out ..." is a strange way of conveying the meaning which has been assigned to it, but it becomes a very simple, clear statement if the location which was called "Titchfield Haven", at that time, was different from the region so named today.

A reduced scale copy was published by Hampshire Field Club of a tracing by Wilberforce Cobbett in 1894 of the Titchfield Estate Map (5). The date of the original map is often stated as 1610 although it is now thought that the date could have been at any time between 1605-10 since it refers to an area as "The copps felled in Anno 1605". The relevant section of this map, Figure 1, indicates a bifurcation of the exit from the estuary with a generally east-going channel in which there are depictions of two single-masted coasting vessels of the time. The east-going branch would be the main river outlet, deflected by the prevailing longshore drift which has built up a spit on the seaward side. The south going branch is probably a breach in the spit caused by scour during periods of high discharge in the river during the winter months; during dry-weather flows in the summer the onshore and longshore movement of gravel by wave action would tend to form a bar at the seaward end which would be scoured away during the next winter. Whilst this variability in depth would preclude the use of this branch for reliable access to the river it could have provided a useful, sheltered mooring area off the main navigable channel, ie. a haven.

The Estate Map specifically refers to the south-going branch as "Titchfield Haven". Later maps apply this designation to the whole of the region upstream of the tidal gates. It appears that the bank which the 3rd Earl had constructed was an extension

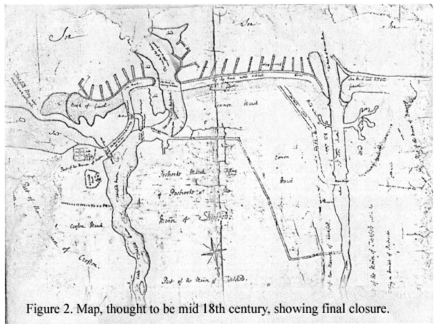

Figure 2. Map, thought to be mid 18th century, showing final closure.

of the end of the spit, which narrowed the exit to a single east-going channel and cut off flow to the south-going branch, identified as "Titchfield Haven". A sketch plan in the Hampshire Records Office of unknown date, but thought to be mid 18th century (Figure 2), indicates this with the remark "The bank first made for shutting out the sea"(6). The statement in the Parish Register now becomes very clear and precise: the south-going branch, known at the time as "Titchfield Haven", was shut out (from the River) thus concentrating the whole flow of the river through the east-going branch. There are several possible reasons for doing this: reclamation, fisheries and to alleviate sedimentation at the entrance.

It is clear that reclamation of the edges of the estuary, particularly in the south-west, was taking place at this time: a lease granted to Richard Tamye in 1614 refers to "...a piece of beech ground lately enclosed and 20 acres of ground lately recovered from the overflowing of the sea, on the west side of the said Haven, aboundeth upon the Com'on of Meane...and upon other the lands of the said Earle lately also recovered from the overflowing of the sea on the North side"(7). This suggests that reclamation had been going on for some time if reclaimed areas were in a state fit to be leased out. It is also interesting that the western boundary was given as Meon Common not as the Canal which would have been the case had it existed at this time. On the mid-18th century plan referred to above there is a dotted line with the remark, "The Bank before the Breach was made": this may be a reclamation bank and the breach may have been made in the great storm of 26 November 1703.

A reason which has been given for the Earl's alleged actions was an assumption that the estuary was silting up. This seems unlikely since chalk streams such as the Meon carry negligible sediment loads into their estuaries; despite passing through Tertiary deposits south of Wickham, the river runs very clear. Also, the waters of the Solent are low in suspended sediment content. There may have been a reduction in mean sea level associated with the long term lowering of temperatures during the "little ice age" but it is likely that the greatest problem affecting navigation in the estuary was, as is still the case today, a partial blockage of the entrance due to continuing extension of the river spit. Closing off the south-going exit would concentrate all flow through the east going channel and would maximise the scouring effect of the out-going flow, to maintain the largest possible channel cross-section to facilitate navigation.

There is a dearth of names relating to fluvial features on the Estate Map: "Titchfield Haven" is one of very few exceptions and relates to a relatively insignificant feature. Since this map was drawn up only a very few years prior to the completion of the works, the 3rd Earl must already have formulated his plans and started on preparations for the work. It seems likely that the identification of this particular feature was a very conscious action.

Richard Tallbotts, who was identified in the Parish Register entry, was apparently from a local family, other members of which appear in the Parish Register. He continued to live within the community, married a local girl in February 1625 and died in April 1629, apparently of natural causes: he was still referred to as "... the Sirvayer of Water Woorkes at Meenelane end...". He was clearly not a Dutchman but, if the construction of the watercourse was much later, Dutch influence could be a possibility.

There are a number of references in Estate account books held in Hampshire Record Office to works carried out on unspecified sluices in the area during the latter half of the 17th century. Sluices and other water engineering works would be essential in land drainage and reclamation; they do not necessarily indicate the presence of a canal.

It is worth noting that there is no reference, direct or indirect, in the Parish Register to the construction of a canal or to any of the many labourers who would have worked on it. Furthermore, there is no reference in the Titchfield Parish Registers up to the year 1763 to any persons involved in the utilisation or maintenance of a canal.

Earl of Southampton's Trust
Under an Indenture dated 18 May 1620 made between the 3rd Earl and a group of 18 Trustees, all inhabitants of Titchfield, properties were leased to the Trustees for 500 years with the intention that they should be utilised in support of employment of the poor in a woollen cloth industry for which "... The Town being situate near the Sea Coast was very commodious...".

It seems inconceivable that the Earl would have made such an investment if, only nine years previously he had been responsible for the closure of the estuary for navigation, and equally improbable that, had he spent huge sums of money on the construction of an innovative canal, he would not have advertised the fact.

Although provision was made in the agreement for replacing the original trustees when they died, this did not appear to take place and the leaseholds eventually devolved to the last surviving trustee, Robert Churcher, and then through a series of his and his descendants' executors to his great-grandson, William Churcher.

Attorney General v William Churcher

On the 9th July 1742, a court action was brought by the Attorney General against William Churcher before the Master of the Rolls. The account of this court action is the most significant piece of evidence that refutes the traditional story that a canal was built for the 3rd Earl of Southampton in 1611; it is very strange that arguments put forward by proponents of the traditional view ignore the existence of these documents entirely!

The Defendant was required to account for the fact that the properties leased by the 3rd Earl had been within the trusteeship of several generations of his family without any of the monies derived from their usage being passed on to the Overseers of the Poor of the Town. At two points in the transcription it states, unequivocally, that the River remained navigable from the Town to the sea and was thereby useful in carrying on the woollen trade to advantage at the demise of the Earl and until the death of his great-grandfather Robert Churcher. He states that at some time after the death of his great-grandfather the River was diverted by the Earl's heirs or assigns "for their benefit" and the consequent loss of the River brought about the rapid and total loss of the woollen trade and a collapse in the revenues derived from it. At no point in his testimony, which covers the period from 1620 to 1742, does he mention the existence of a canal facilitating waterborne transport between the Town and the sea. This testimony was given under oath and accepted by the two leading judicial officers in the country.

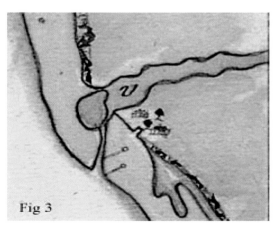
Fig 3

The 3rd Earl of Southampton died 10 November 1624 and Robert Churcher was buried on 4 June 1643; this would put the earliest possible date for the diversion of the River in the second half of the 17th century. Support for this conclusion appears in the history of a lease granted to the Stares family for "Meene Farm". The acreage of the property decreased at some time after it was referred to in a survey of 1632 due, according to a letter written in 1756 from Clement Walcot, the Receiver to the Duke of Portland for his Hampshire Estates, to John Lucas of the Inner Temple, London, to the cutting of the New River.

Evidence from Naval Charts

The charts of Greenvile Collins (1693-8) and Dummer & Wiltshaw (1698-9) utilise conventions for displaying the mouths of rivers and streams which are clear and totally consistent. They show the high and low water lines. They do not show the courses of freshwater streams either in the intertidal zone or inland of the high water mark and, possibly, for this reason do not show the New River. They do not show the presence of a canal but indicate that the entrance to the estuary was still open and navigable, even including navigation marks; this would be surprising if the New River was a navigable watercourse. They name the lower part of the estuary as "Titchfield Lake". This does not necessarily indicate a body of fresh water since the term "Lake" is frequently used on charts of this area for naming navigable tidal channels; there are several examples of this usage in Portsmouth and Langstone Harbours. At the mouth of the estuary there is a detached area of land which may be the area of reclamation previously referred to. There is a narrow channel, connecting to Titchfield Lake, separating the area of land from the western high water mark, which appears to be crossed by a structure which looks like a bridge but may incorporate a sluice gate; the channel does not appear to flow continuously as it has not cut through the intertidal zone. The reason for this narrow channel is not clear; it may have been part of the drainage of the reclaimed area or it may contain one of the three flood hatches whose presence is stated in a schedule of works dated 174010. It is possible that this channel formed a weak point which led to the later breach. A detail of the Dummer & Wiltshaw chart of 1698 is shown here in Figure 3. The area identified as "v" is named as Titchfield Lake.

The earliest cartographic representation of the New River, so far discovered, is a chart by Joseph Avery of 173111, which clearly shows the watercourse, but does not name it, with the Breech and the original river exit to the East closed off. The watercourse is referred to in 1740 in a letter from Clement Walcot to John Lucas, concerning land boundaries 12, as the New River, not the Canal. This letter also identifies the structure at the lower end of the watercourse as hatches, not as a sea-lock; this term being used consistently on a number of sketch maps drawn by Clement Walcot during the 1740s. It contains further items of interest such as the reference to clap gates, probably an early form of the tidal flaps at the head of the present harbour at Hill Head.

Other Accounts

There are two other accounts of interest, both by past Vicars of Titchfield. On 13th May 1899, the Hampshire Chronicle carried a report on a visit by members of The Hampshire Field Club to Hill Head, in which the Rev. R. A. R. White was quoted:

"... they were standing on what was one of the largest earthworks in Hampshire - all the ground for some distance was artificial. The valley was at one time tidal, and there was nothing but a sea route, Titchfield itself being in those days a little seaport. There was an old map belonging to the Delmé family, formerly hanging in Cams Hall, on which ships were shown alongside the road leading to Gosport, which crossed the valley close up to Titchfield, while local tradition asserted that ships went up as far as Place House. When the monasteries were dissolved the trade of Titchfield decreased very rapidly; then the Earls tried what they could to revive the trade, and started woollen manufactories, which failed. Then they taught the children of the poor to weave, but that failed, and then they thought of a great work to encourage agriculture - they erected that earthwork, put in flood gates, and reclaimed the land for two and a half miles inland to Titchfield, and it was now valuable grazing land." This account supports the general chronology proposed above and does not include any reference to the existence of a canal at any time.

In a little history of St Peter's Church, published in the late 1940s, the Vicar of Titchfield from 1936 - 47, the Rev. Frank Edward Spurway stated: "The river-mouth was closed in the reign of Charles II," ie between 1660 - 1685. Unfortunately the Rev Spurway does not state his evidence for this statement but a recent discovery, by Keith Hayward, in a volume of presentments at the Manorial Court of Titchfield in 1676 includes two complaints by residents of Posbrooke that the acreages of their copyholds had been reduced by the cutting of the New River. This suggests that the New River had been completed or was in an advanced stage of construction by that time. The Lord of the Manor responsible would have been Edward Noel, the 1st Earl of Gainsborough.

The 3rd Earl of Southampton's second son succeeded to the title in 1624 and died in 1667 leaving no male heir to continue the Earldom. His estates were divided up in 1669 between his three daughters; Titchfield went to Elizabeth Wriothesley, (1636-80), eldest daughter of the 4th Earl, who married Edward

Noel, 1st Earl of Gainsborough.
It is interesting to note that Rachell Vahan (2nd daughter of the 4th Earl of Southampton) married William Russell on 10th August 1669. This was her second marriage; William, Lord Russell was the 3rd son of the 4th Earl (1st Duke) of Bedford. Three generations of the Earls of Bedford had considerable interests in the major drainage works in the Fens carried out by the Dutchman Cornelius Vermuyden culminating in the completion of the Bedford New River in 1651.

William may have encouraged his brother-in-law Edward Noel to carry out the extensive water engineering works at Titchfield, including the New River and the local tradition of Dutch involvement in the enterprise may suggest that one of the Dutch engineers brought over by Vermuyden planned and supervised the work.

When was the first reference to it being a canal?
The earliest instances of the terms Titchfield Canal and Sea Lock have not been established but White's Directory of 1859, when describing the watercourse, states that it was "chiefly for the purpose of drainage and irrigation, and not now used for the navigation of barges". This is not proof that the New River was built originally for that purpose.

In other parts of the country, such as the Somerset Levels and the Fens, man-made channels have been utilised for local transport of produce even though this was not their original purpose, eg. peat for fuel, osiers for basketry and reeds for thatching, and indigenous watercraft have been developed such as the Somerset Turf Boat and the Withy Boat of the Cambridgeshire Fens, usually propelled by poling or tracking.

There is anecdotal evidence that farmers in the upper reaches of the River Meon utilised the river for the transport of farm produce. Water meadows required considerable maintenance and it is quite likely that the New River was used for the transport of men, tools and materials between them and Titchfield Village and perhaps for carrying the hay from the meadows.

Conclusions.
There is not one shred of evidence to support the traditionally held views regarding the origin and purpose of the New River; any such views are based totally upon speculation, unless any real evidence is discovered to support them.

Proponents of these traditional views seem to totally ignore any evidence which contradicts their idée fixe.

The available evidence suggests that the 3rd Earl of Southampton was not responsible for shutting off the mouth of the Meon from the sea, causing the cessation of maritime trade to the town of Titchfield, nor for the construction of a canal. His action, reported in the Register for 1611, was to facilitate reclamation within the estuary of the river and possibly to maintain the main navigable channel. Evidence indicates that the river remained navigable from Titchfield to the sea up until at least the second half of the 17th century. The reason that considerable effort by many local historians has failed to unearth any evidence relating to a canal constructed for the 3rd Earl is simply that no such canal ever existed; it appears that, from the available evidence, this watercourse, called The New River, was constructed in the latter half of the 17th century by the 1st Earl of Gainsborough to facilitate the extension of the reclamation of the western side of the estuary and was eventually used to supply the extensive water meadows developed over this area.

John Mitchell

References.
1. Fareham Borough Council. A Local Biodiversity Action Plan for Fareham.
2. Hayward, K.ed., 1998. Titchfield Parish Register 1589-1634. Titchfield History Society.
3. Earl of Southamptons Grant of Severall Lands &c to the Towne of Titchfield for 500 years dated 18th May 1620. Archives of Earl of Southampton's Trust.
4. Copy of Order on Hearing of Attorney General against Churcher dated 9th July 1742. Archives of Earl of Southampton's Trust.
5. Hants Field Club, 1894. The Titchfield Estate,From A XVIIth Century Map. Reprinted 1983. Winchester: Hampshire Field Club.
6. Hampshire Record Office 1M46/1. Plan of Titchfield Haven, 18th Century.
7. Hampshire Record Office 5M53/331.
8. Collins, Capt. Greenvile. 1693. Chart of the Solent, including the coast of Hampshire and the Isle of Wight in Great Britain's Coasting Pilot.
9. Dummer, E. and Wiltshaw, Capt. T., 1698. Chart of The River of Southampton in A Survey of Ports on the Southwest Coast of England from Dover to the Lands-end.
10. Hampshire Record Office 5M53/1110/51. A Particular of ye Repairs at Hillhead.
11. Avery, J. 1731. Chart of The Sea Coasts from Arundel to St Albans, including The Solent and coast of Hampshire.
12.Hampshire Record Office 5M53/1110/9.

THE OLD SLUICE AT HILL HEAD HARBOUR

Titchfield Haven was shut out at the costs of the 3rd Earl of Southampton on 23 June 1611 according the Parish Register of that year. As part of this work it is assumed that a sluice was constructed under the shingle bank to permit the river to continue to run out to the sea. This is shown in a map (HRO 1M46/1), but which is not dated, a detail from which is shown on page 70 (East is uppermost).

The shingle bank which now forms the western side of Hill Head harbour is shown to have an "old sluice" close to its mid-point and a new sluice closer to the shore. The new sluice has been renewed and is currently used to permit the river to run out at low tide. The old sluice has been closed off at its harbour side. Both these sluices can be seen today.

The old sluice was last used in the late 1940's whilst the gates on the new sluice were replaced over a period of several months. The old sluice was subsequently blocked on the harbour side.

As part of general research on the local area a group has been formed to investigate the history. The *GATHER* (**G**roup **A**cquiring **T**itchfield **H**aven **E**arly **R**ecords) group was formed in October 2007 and one of its earliest studies has been to examine the old sluice.

From the marsh side the old sluice is approached by a water filled gully about 2m wide which then enters a tunnel under the road over the old shingle bank. This is believed to be the gully with the left-angled leg shown on the closure map (Fig 1). The water in the gully was only a few inches deep but covered about 3ft of mud and silt. There were a number of old planks close to the entrance which were probably left behind when the sluice was damaged in about 1980.

A small dinghy was used to get into the sluice which was examined on 15 November 2007. Since the sluice was built to Imperial units these are used to define its dimensions, although metric equivalents are given in [brackets].

Figure 2

The sluice is 92in [2340mm] wide. The lower part (culvert) is built using dressed stone about 10in [250mm] wide which appeared to be old (maybe 1600's). Depth soundings in the culvert indicted that the water was about 36in [915mm] deep, although the lower 30in [75mm] was thick mud partly filled with debris (old planks and stones). The bottom appeared to be level and hard, suggesting it was made of stone.

The top arch of the sluice is built using bricks (8¾in long, 4in wide & 2in deep). These look thin compared to modern bricks and may be as old as the stones. The cement appears to be original and not to have been refaced in recent times. The outer edge of the brick arch is in a poor condition and there is a danger that a further collapse may occur. The bank around the arch is covered in hedging and bushes which line the road above. The road is only about 30in [760mm] above the top of the arch.

The water level in the sluice on the day it was examined was about

Figure 3

6in [150mm] below OS datum. This was assessed by measuring the water height at the new sluice against an OS Benchmark on the bridge. The old sluice is connected to the river, although the gully is overgrown with reed beds. The water level in the river changes slightly with rainfall amounts, although on the day in question it was judged to be at a typical height.

The harbour end of the tunnel has been filled with concrete. It is understood that this was done in about 1985 when work-men digging a trench for a pipe from Meon shore along the road broke through into the sluice. As an expedient the hole and tunnel below were filled and this will prevent the sluice being used again.

Historical Footnote:
As mentioned, the closure map (Fig.1) is not dated. It shows at the top (south) that a breach occurred in the sea bank at some time. It is surmised that after a prolonged rainy period the water in the river Meon rose to a level that the old sluice was unable to discharge adequately. Correspondingly, the high water level forced the breach in the sea bank. It was therefore necessary to construct a larger new sluice. The earliest record of such activities is in a letter by Clement Walcott (HRO 5M53/1115) in 1743, in which he refers to the need to locally dig clay for repairs to Hill Head. A map prepared when the estate was sold to the Delme's in 1753 (HRO 21M53) indicates that there was not a breach in the sea bank and that both sluices were operating. This is confirmed in a subsequent map by Archer & Pitts dated 1774 (in British Library), but apparently the old sluice was not in operation in 1837 as indicated by the Titchfield Parish Tithe map.

It is therefore apparent that the old sluice predated 1743 and it is very likely that it was built at the same time that the estuary was closed in 1611. That is, that the stonework is about 400 years old. The brick arch may have been repaired later but a sluice covering a height of 100in [2.5m] above the river level would have been necessary to prevent overtopping by high spring tides on the harbour side.

John C Lewthwaite

THE SEA LOCK

At the southern end of the Titchfield Canal there is supposedly a sea lock which was used to permit barges to enter the canal from waiting ships moored in the entrance from the sea.

The view today is shown by this photograph taken from the canal side with the seaward side beyond.

The water level on the canal side is controlled upstream by a sluice. The seaward side is very overgrown and closed to the sea.

The three-arched bridge is a later addition and covers where the lock was apparently installed. A local information board on the east side reports that the area in Grade II listed and was restored in 1994. It describes the old lock as a pair of simple staunch gates which could only be opened when the water level on both sides was the same.

The area was examined in June 2008. The width where the bridge is fitted is 16ft (5.0m). The water depth was 3ft (0.9m) deep and this is relatively constant since there are drains under the road on the seaward side which empty into the marsh. The bottom was probed from the bridge and the side banks and found to be hard and level (stoned lined ?). Remains of iron-work type fittings can still be discerned on the seaward side, indicated by the line

It is not clear whether the lock gates were designed to swing inwards from the sea or outwards from the canal. Nor it is clear as to how the gates could be secured against a head of water from either side. An old Ordnance Survey map (dated 1941) shows a Bench Mark on the road over bridge at a height of 7.53ft (2.3m).

Since the road over the bridge is 3.3ft (1.0m) above the water, this indicates that the water level is currently about 4.3ft (1.3m) above the OS datum. The datum is the mean level of tides which locally range about +/- 5.9ft (1.8m) on Neaps to +/- 7.9ft

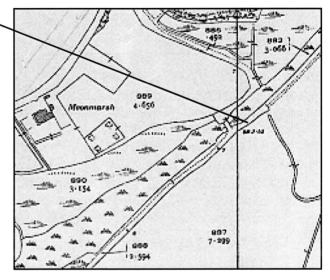

(2.4m) on Spring tides.These relevant heights are shown below assuming that the sea lock is closed: If the entrance were still open to the sea, the water on the seaward side of the lock on Spring tides with a height of 7.9ft (2.4m)

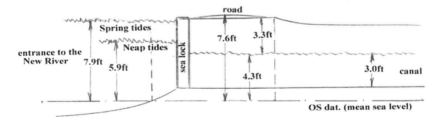

relative to the OS datum, would tend to flood over the bridge and lock sides to a depth of about 0.3ft (0.1m)! However, data from the Inter-government Panel for Climate Change suggests that sea levels were about 1ft lower 300 to 400 years ago. It should also be noted that the range of Spring tides in those years was little different from today. So it may be concluded that the maximum height of tide probably did not quite reach the top of the lock sides all those years ago.

Observations also indicates that the height of the road leading from the lock to Meon Shore is about 0.6ft lower than that over the bridge and hence on Spring tides 300 to 400 years ago, the maximum height of the tide would have been very close to the present road level. It might therefore be concluded that there must have been a raised bank where the road now runs.

We know that the lock was open to the sea from the "closure map" (HRO 1M 46/1- which is not dated), a section of which is shown on page 70 (East is uppermost). The waterway is called the "New River", the bridge is clearly marked by the words "Meon bridge" and the road is entitled "sea bank called Hill Head".It can be seen that the word "sluice" is shown on this map, rather than lock.

If there had been a simple staunch lock then it would have had to be able to withstand a head of water of about 3.3ft (1.0m) either on the canal side at low tide, or a similar height from the seaward side on Spring tides. The load imposed on a 16ft (5.0m) wide structure has been calculated to be about 2.5tons force ! It would seem unlikely that the ironwork hinges would have withstood such loads.

The concept of opening the staunch gate lock only when the water levels were the same, is hardly practical since the tide would have been rising steadily relative to the canal level, leaving only a few minutes of operation. With any difference in water levels, a significant current would develop making it very difficult to close the gates.

Furthermore, if the gates were not closed on Spring tides the water level in the canal would have been raised by about 3.3ft (1.0m) all the way up to Titchfield, probably flooding over adjacent fields. Since this inflow was from the sea, this would have contaminated the area with salt water.

It is therefore concluded that a single "staunch" lock would be impractical at this point. A more controllable structure would have been constructed such as a sluice, as indicated on the "closure" map, which could be partly opened to allow water to flow out of the canal as desired at low tide. Such an arrangement would of course preclude the passage of barges from the sea into the canal.

It might be postulated that ships could be moored alongside on the seaward side of the sluice and similarly barges on the canal side, with goods being transported across by cart. However, there was a well defined track from the sea lock to Titchfield (as shown on the 1610 map), so why not transport such goods directly from the sea lock by road? In any case, such goods would have had to have been off-loaded from the barges at Titchfield and distributed by cart – so what advantage did the canal offer? And there are no obvious landing quays on either side of the lock.

It has therefore been concluded, that there wasn't a simple staunch lock at this location since the concept is impractical mainly because of water height differences. There was almost certainly a sluice as indicated on the "closure" map. Such a sluice would have prevented craft from entering the canal. Small ships could have used the new sea entrance and distributed their goods by road. Perhaps the canal was simply a drainage/irrigation ditch.

John C Lewthwaite

TITCHFIELD HAVEN AND NEW RIVER

A booklet entitled 'The parish church of St Peter, Titchfield'[1] states anonymously that "the river mouth was closed in the reign of Charles II and a canal was dug from the sea to where the old tanyard stood". In 1742, during a court case concerning the Earl of Southampton's Charity, it was reported that "circumstances had been greatly altered by reason of the loss of the river, which at the Earl's demise was navigable from the sea to the town and therefore very useful in carrying on the woollen trade. This channel had however been diverted by the Earl's heirs for their benefit, and the woollen trade had been totally lost"[2]. In a letter of 1752, the estate agent Clement Walcot refers to a change in the area of land leased to the Stares family, supposing that the land was originally surveyed "before the New River was made"[3].

The original lease goes back to the 1640s. It has been stated that the New River was built in 1614, but the source of this information is not given.[4]Under 24th June 1611 the Parish Register states that "the same day Titchfield Haven was shutt out by one Richard Talbotts industrie under gods permisione at the costs of the right honorable the Earle of Southampton".[5]

On 14th April 1629 Richard Talbutt "the Sirvayer of Water Woorkes at Meenelane end" was buried.[6] A lease to Richard Tamye dated 6th June 1614 includes inter alia 20 acres of land "lately recovered from the overflowing of the sea".

[7] These last three statements can reasonably be linked to the construction of the sea wall, but no reference to the construction of a two-mile watercourse from the village to the sea can be construed from them.

The Tamye lease supports the idea that the purpose of the sea wall was land reclamation.With such distant and imprecise testimony as this mostly is, small wonder that it has proved so difficult to determine the origins of the New River. However, on 4th October 1676 a volume of presentments at the Manorial Court of Titchfield[8] included the following recently discovered entries:"Wee p'sent that ye Lord of this mannor by Cutting ye new River hath taken away & doth detaine one acre of Land from John Cooper which belongeth to his Coppiehold. Also wee p'sent that ye said Lord doth detaine Two acres of Land from John Landy which belongeth to his Coppiehold, Taken away by Cutting ye said new River." These entries provide four new pieces of information: a new and firm terminus ante quem for the construction of the New River; it was the Lord of the Manor that did it, and the names of two people whose land was adversely affected by its construction.

However, questions still remain. Neither the reason for its construction, nor the date, are given, but at the risk of inferring from insufficient data one might suppose that a tenant would complain promptly about the severance of his land and not wait years to do so.

That suggests a construction date in the early to mid-1670s, which would also be consistent with the first three references quoted above.

However, it would be unwise to make a more definite assertion until more evidence emerges.

References:

[1] Hampshire Record Office TOP313/1/4

[2] Smith, D.G.: Four centuries of the Earl of Southampton Trust, The Trust, 1997, pp 8-9

[3] H.R.O. 5M53/1129/43

[4] Everard, M.: Water meadows, Forrest, 2005, p.207

[5] H.R.O. 37M73/PR1

[6] H.R.O. 37M73/PR17 HRO 5M53/331-3328 HRO 16M63/14

Keith Hayward

THE CLOSURE OF TITCHFIELD HAVEN

The town of Titchfield has had a long association with the sea and it was a small, but thriving, port connected to the Solent by, firstly the River Meon and, secondly, by a man-made water channel. There is no written history of the origin of this water channel, which is now known as the Titchfield Canal but, however, it is there for all to see. It is 2 miles long (3000 metres), between 16ft. and 20ft. (5 metres) wide and, originally, the water channel would have been a minimum of between 6ft. and 7ft. (2 metres) deep (there would have been between 2ft. and 3ft. of 'freeboard' above the level of water, as in all canals). The path of the canal is relatively straight, with few bends. The amount of material which would have been removed in the building of the canal has been calculated to be approximately 30000 cubic metres, equating to about 60000 tonnes of soil/aggregate.

With the very limited technology available until the Industrial Revolution, and the lower physical stature of the general populace, it is estimated that, at the time of the building of the canal, it would take 100 men one year to dig out and distribute that amount, by hand. This takes into account both the vagaries of the weather and the lack of daylight hours in the winter. In the 17th Century, there would not have been that number of available able-bodied men in the whole of the Parish of Titchfield, so a smaller number over a longer period is more likely, mostly sub-contracted from outside the district. Using modern costs, and allowing for overheads, this has been calculated as the equivalent to an outlay of between £2m and £3m. Why is there no record of this significantly large amount of monetary outlay, or the employment of the workforce?

We have, however, two records, from the period which contain facts of relevance to the situation in Titchfield Haven in the early 1600s; the Titchfield Parish Registers and the 1605/10 map of the Titchfield Manorial Estate. An earlier record states that John Leland, the renowned antiquary, visited Titchfield in 1542 and wrote that, below Warebridge (identified as the river bridge on Bridge Street) the river ebith and floweth; so was tidal. The Parish Registers state that, in June 1611, Titchfield Haven was shutt out by one Richard Talbotts, at the costs of the Earle of Southampton; this was Henry Wriothesley, the 3rd Earl of Southampton (1573-1624). The inhabitants of Titchfield Parish would have witnessed the sea coming in, up close to the town, twice a day, and then disappearing again as the tide went out. The area over which this apparent phenomenon happened is called Titchfield Haven, and the reasonable interpretation of 'shutt out' is that it refers to the sea as being shut out. There is some evidence that the passage from the sea to Titchfield had a very difficult entrance/exit to the sea, was not easily navigable from there to the town, and it has been suggested that silting-up might have been an increasing problem.

A further reference in the Parish Registers states that a Richard Talbutt died in 1629, and he was described as the Sirvayer of Water Woorkes at Meene lane end. 'Meene lane end' can be interpreted as the end of the lane through the hamlet of Meon, which is exactly where the present sea-lock exists, and 'Water Woorkes' is one way of describing a sea-lock incorporated into a waterway system which, later, will be seen to have some significance.

The 1605/10 map of the Titchfield Manorial Estate has been researched recently and is, in all probability, genuine. It can be shown that the mathematical knowledge in the early 17th Century was sufficiently advanced to produce such an accurate map; this mathematical/engineering knowledge would, also, have been necessary in closing the estuary, and building a Canal New River. The 3rd Earl of Southampton was, as has been established, associated with at least two of the leading scientists and mathematicians of the day, Henry Briggs and Edward Wright, and they would have been available to him for providing the essential expertise.

The map in Figure 1 is a detail from the 1605/10 map and shows the Meon Estuary at low tide with no canal. The shingle bank is clearly seen, resulting

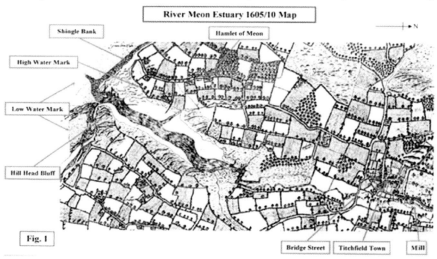

89

in a narrow exit to the sea, and the river bifurcates outside the Estuary in the littoral region below the high tide mark, and amalgamates with the Solent. At high tide, this bifurcation would have been covered with water, and it is not known whether the shingle bank was covered; Figure 2 shows the river mouth at both low and high tide, and the existence of the shingle bank emphasises the narrow entrance to the Haven, which would even more hazardous if the shingle bank were covered at high tide. The distance from Meon Lane End to the Hill Head bluff is approximately 600 metres, and this is the minimum length of the barrier necessary to close off the estuary. The existence of the shingle bank would have been of great benefit to the construction engineers, and the higher the bank was above the low tide mark, the less in-fill material would be needed to complete he barrier. As will be explained later, the closure of the Haven would have been a lengthy exercise, probably costing far more than the sum, calculated above, to build the canal.

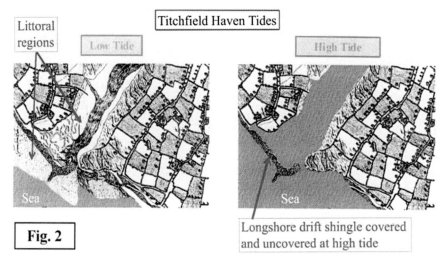

Littoral regions

Titchfield Haven Tides

Low Tide

High Tide

Sea

Sea

Fig. 2

Longshore drift shingle covered and uncovered at high tide

Until recently, the commonly held belief was that the 3rd Earl of Southampton built the canal in conjunction with closing the estuary. The lack of documentary evidence has caused this assumption to be questioned, together with references, through various sources of a later period, to land associated with a 'New River'. On these later documents there is nothing to identify to where on the river they referred; the term 'New River' was used for man-made extensions to the River Meon system well outside the canal area. Another commonly held opinion was that the estuary was closed in order to reclaim valuable land from the sea which, on closer engineering examination, can be shown to be an impossibility, except for very small parcels of land in certain peripheral parts of the littoral area, to be explained later.

There is much evidence that Titchfield was a fairly busy, if small, port, and it can be argued, effectively, that Henry, the 3rd Earl of Southampton had every incentive to keep the port open. He was an early industrialist with a great interest in Virginia and the East Indies. He had Iron Mills at Titchfield and Beaulieu (also, he had plans for using Botley Mill). Continuing the export of wool and leather products and the import of goods (wine, for instance) was still a high priority, and frequent visits to the Isle of Wight, where he was Governor, would have been important; the plying of ships to and from London, and along the whole of the south coast, might have been equally relevant. Also, social visits to both Beaulieu and the Isle of Wight were important, especially if they involved Royalty, or other important people. All of the above indicates that having a channel open to enable vessels, whatever they might have been, to travel up to Titchfield would have pre-eminence amongst the 3rd Earl's industrial, and private, projects.

A case has been made, therefore, for the 3rd Earl to build a canal, but what are the alternatives? An interesting factual observation is that, in order to build the Titchfield Canal it is not necessary to close the Haven. Therefore, the fundamental question that can be asked is, why did he close the Haven? The conclusion sheds a new light on the whole Titchfield Canal enigma.

Firstly, we must consider the problem of how did Richard Talbot (modern spelling), possibly under the direction of engineers, Henry Briggs or Edward Wright, set about closing an estuary over a distance of 600/700 metres, using the rudimentary tools, and techniques, which were available at the start of the 17th Century. After much discussion with the engineering fraternity, it is concluded that there would have been only one practical method of creating a barrier 4 metre wide and 1.5 metres above the maximum high water mark, which is considered to be sufficiently robust to withstand the most severe of storms normally encountered in the Solent. This would be by, firstly, in-filling the deepest level, which was the main exit to the sea at the Hill Head bluff until the land level at that point was at the same height as the shingle bank and, then, progressively in-filling upwards, until the estuary was closed. Obviously, by gradually increasing the height over which the water flows during each tide, an ever larger lake is formed inside the estuary as low tide approached, and the level of sea-water dropped below the in-fill height. The addition of the layers could be undertaken at the speed of availability of in-filling material, but it is obvious that it would, quite quickly, restrict the draft of ships which could enter the Haven, and the size of the lake, so formed, would increase in depth with each infill. This method would be the only choice for the restricted technology of the 17th Century. Finally, a lake was formed inside the Haven, which would be approximately the size of the previous water area at high tide; the water enclosed in the lake would have been part sea water and part fresh water. An approximation of the lake formed in the estuary is indicated in Figure 3, shown overlaid on top of a modern satellite photograph; the outline approximates to the high water mark of the 1605/10 map but, clearly, the actual lake would have been different in detail. There might well have been some land reclamation, as mentioned above, which would have been relatively easy without the daily two tides, and there would have been some areas of the peripheries of the lake which were shallow enough to allow easy closing off to form dry land.

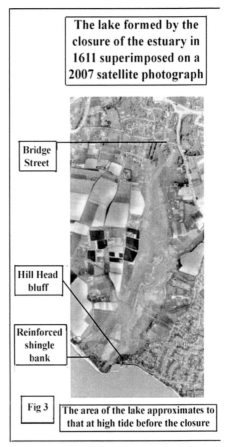

The lake formed by the closure of the estuary in 1611 superimposed on a 2007 satellite photograph

Bridge Street

Hill Head bluff

Reinforced shingle bank

Fig 3 The area of the lake approximates to that at high tide before the closure

It has been substantiated that a lake would have been formed behind the barrier of the closure, and this would be fed by the main River Meon, the various tributaries within the estuary, run-off surface water from the surrounding countryside and sea water, both deliberately introduced and during the inclement weather periods, especially high south-west winds, to which the Solent is occasionally exposed. To compensate for this, not inconsequential, constant ingress of water, it would be necessary to insert a controllable sluice/lock system allowing excess water to flow out into the sea which, in consequence, would keep the height of the Titchfield Lake well below the closure barrier height. The lack of a road system at Hill Head Bluff, and the potential engineering difficulties associated with the tidal race at that point, the western end would be a favourite location. Referring to figure 4, the closure of the estuary has been completed, a sluice/lock introduced along the shingle bank, towards the Meon Lane End area and exiting directly onto the beach. As seen above, the Parish Register relates that a Richard Talbutt died in 1629, and he was described as the Sirvayer of Water Woorkes at Meene lane end. The assumption has already been made that this refers to our Richard Talbot, who was a man of some consequence, having organised the unique closure of a substantial haven, demonstrating his outstanding engineering skills. The term 'Surveyor' was given to such eminent figures as Henry Briggs, Edward Wright, William Oughtred, Edmund Gunter and other leading mathematicians of the age, and it is not unreasonable to conclude that the 'Water Works' referred to had some significance, justifying the continued employment of a man of such worth; there had to be a sluice/lock, and there was a Water Works at Meon Lane End, and it is difficult to imagine that they were not one and the same. The lock as shown in Figure 4 would have been quite rudimentary in operation and, it can be argued, that it was not necessary to employ Richard Talbot to look after it; we have to suggest more realistic alternatives.

Returning to the need of the Earl to maintain a port at Titchfield, the existence of a large lake, equivalent to high tide conditions in the Haven, would enable shipping to be used continuously between the closing barrier and the Town. Inevitably, the sluice/lock would need to be far more complicated than that suggested so far, but Henry Wriothesley, and his engineers, would have been able to obtain details of the type of lock which was being used on the Exeter Canal, the first canal to be built in the British Isles in the post-Roman period, which had been completed some 40 years earlier; reports state that the lock used in Exeter was a pound' lock which

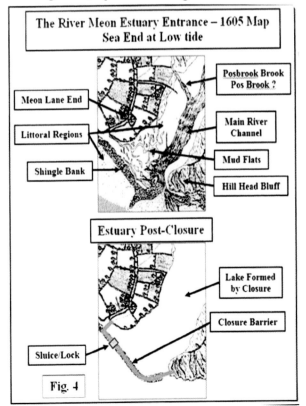

The River Meon Estuary Entrance – 1605 Map
Sea End at Low tide

Posbrook Brook
Pos Brook ?

Meon Lane End

Main River Channel

Littoral Regions

Mud Flats

Shingle Bank

Hill Head Bluff

Estuary Post-Closure

Lake Formed by Closure

Closure Barrier

Sluice/Lock

Fig. 4

93

had never before been used in this Country. Such a lock would increase the importance of the 'water works' and further justify Richard Talbot as the surveyor. The use of a pound lock would extend, considerably, the period of time over which ships could enter the lake, especially if a relatively deep channel were created running from the lock to the sea, and thus, considering the advantages gained, the Earl would have a far more satisfactory access to the Port of Titchfield than previously. We have, therefore, found a very plausible reason as to why Henry Wriothesley closed out the Haven in 1611, which is far superior to the alternatives. For instance, desiring to have a lake for wild fowl 'conservation' for hunting, possibly allied to extending fish stocks, or that the possession of a large lake, subjected to conservative landscaping, would enhance his reputation and Estate, and impress those who need impressing (James I, for instance). It is difficult to see the economic justification for these other concepts, but extravagant follies undertaken by the aristocracy were far from unknown.

Existing sluice/lock at Meon Lane End is, clearly, associated with a later period in the canal's history, and we have no records of what was put in position in 1611; it is interesting to consider possible alternatives as to where the first lock was positioned, and some possibilities as to where the shipping channel was located. From Figure 4, it can be seen that the position of the lock is not a favourable position for a shipping channel; examination of the littoral area inshore from the shingle bank shows a marshy and shallow area which would probably be unsuitable for the shipping channel. In Figure 5 the sluice/lock has been moved to approximately where the current lock is situated, with a channel to the sea, as would have been used for the canal when it was in operation. The shipping channel shown in the first drawing, avoids the marshy

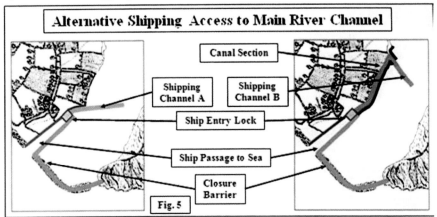

Alternative Shipping Access to Main River Channel

Canal Section

Shipping Channel A

Shipping Channel B

Ship Entry Lock

Ship Passage to Sea

Closure Barrier

Fig. 5

area mentioned previously, and joins the main river course. The second drawing utilises the current path of the canal up to where the Posbrook Brook (Pos Brook?) enters the Haven, using the path of this stream for the shipping route. These suggestions are conjecture only, and there is no evidence of any validity, but they illustrate that the lower canal could have been built by the 3rd Earl and feeding into the main river channel.

Examination of the urban part of the canal, between Bridge Street and Titchfield Mill, shows that that part of the canal is about 6 metres wide along much of its length, and those parts which are less in width can be seen to be overgrown, due to build-up of the banks by silt and vegetation, the result of poor maintenance, and could have accommodated small sea-going ships of the 17th and 18th Centuries. This urban section could have been built at the time of the 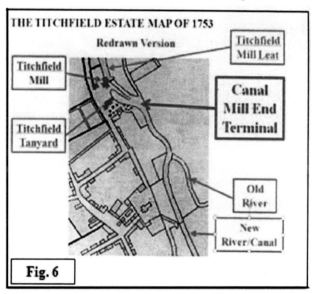 Haven Closure, and joined to the main river in, or to the south of, the Bridge Street area. There is a later map of the Titchfield Estate, dated 1753, showing this urban section, which is included in Figure 6 together with a redrawn version, helping to clarify the details; comparing this map with current maps of the area show that it was drawn to a considerably high level of cartographic accuracy. One interpretation of these details is that there is plenty of room to sail, or tow, small sea-going ships, a berthing area and, it can be argued, room for them to be turned around. Once again, there is no written record of the building of this part of the canal, but it would have been very much in the Earl's interest to have this part of the canal in place.

If further evidence is needed to prove that a lake filled the majority of the estuary on the closing off, a survey of the current topography and terrain is sufficient. The estuary is 2 miles long and between 1/4mile and 1/2 mile in

95

width, and the land level is completely flat at, or just above, mean high water mark; a study of geology will tell one that this is indicative of silt deposit associated with river flooding. What is currently visible along the length of the estuary are meadows of a swampy nature, with no evidence of arable farming, along which flows the remains of the original River Meon, interspersed by small and larger lakes, especially towards the sea. Flooding still takes place in the upper reaches of the estuary and in the water meadows further upstream; measurements of the actual amount of silt deposited during these flood periods varies from year to year but, typically, of the order of 10mm or 20mm, although the winter of 2010/11 has produced over 50mm of deposit along the banks of the leat to Titchfield Mill. Having established that the River Meon is a silt bearing river, and as there is little reason to believe that it was not, also, silt bearing in the 17th Century, it can be seen that it would not take many years for the flooded closed-off estuary to silt up along the peripheries, the mud flats and the main littoral area of the original estuary and, inevitably, into the main shipping channel. This would have the effect of reducing the size of the lake, affecting the passage of ships, if that were still taking place, and it can be postulated that the silting-up could be seen to be effective within 30 years of the closure; there would be much further deposit over the years before the levels reach those seen currently. When the lake became too silted-up to allow the easy passage of ships is not known but, it is considered that this could easily have been so by 1660. If the canal were not built shortly after the closure of Titchfield Haven, the silting-up of the lake within the estuary could be cited as a reason why it was built, or why the two ends were joined together. It is thought possible that, as the silting-up became worse, the canal at the top and bottom ends was added to, in fairly short lengths, over a period of some years. Examination of the existing canal shows that there is some indication of variation in topography along its length, which might indicate that it was not completed in one piece, but this appearance could be due to variable maintenance on various portions of the canal.

It would be interesting to find out what had happened for other closures of estuaries but, so far, only one has been located. That is the closure of the river Wansbeck, in Northumberland in 1975, and they were under the impression that they were the first in the UK. They inserted a barrier about 500 metres upstream from the mouth of the estuary, and a lake has been formed upstream, over a distance of about 2 miles; the barrier includes a pound lock and a sluice to enable excess water to be discharged. Obviously, the engineering methods used were of the 20th Century, but the effect over the estuary was exactly the same as in Titchfield in 1611, and it is interesting to record that they are, already, suffering from problems of silting, but the use of the closed river for navigation is minimal.

A further point to be discussed is whether an Act of Parliament would have been required for the closure; a considerable portion of land was to be acquired by the landowner, Henry Wriothesley, the 3rd. Earl of Southampton. An Act of Parliament was required before the Exeter Canal was built, and this procedure continued for subsequent developments of a similar nature. Because there is no record of an Act of Parliament it must be assumed that Royal permission was received, without any written confirmation. The 3rd Earl of Southampton was seen to have the favour of James 1 and it has to be assumed that he obtained a special grant from the King. The next King, Charles I came to the throne shortly after Henry Wriothesley died, and his son made no contact with Royalty for some years, leaving his mother to oversee the Titchfield Estate. The build up to the Civil War commenced during this time, and it difficult to see that the closure of estuaries, and the building of canals had any precedence in daily affairs. Also, it is impossible to see that any permission would have been granted during the Commonwealth period, and subsequently, for the work at Titchfield to be undertaken without an Act of Parliament. The conclusion is that the 3rd Earl of Southampton was, uniquely, able to close the estuary, and build a canal, albeit in small portions. It has been established, clearly, that he closed the Titchfield Haven, but whether he built a canal is open to conjecture, but a case has been made. The position of the canal on the 1605/10 map is indicated in Figure 7.

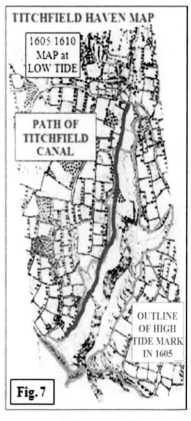

TITCHFIELD HAVEN MAP

1605 1610 MAP at LOW TIDE

PATH OF TITCHFIELD CANAL

OUTLINE OF HIGH TIDE MARK IN 1605

Fig. 7

After much due consideration, it is thought that the suggestion that the 3rd Earl closed the Haven, in order to use it as an improved shipping channel, to keep open the Port of Titchfield, is the only one which has a financially viable

97

essence and, hence, is the most likely reason. However, we have no documentary evidence, other than the Parish Records, and the topographical evidence of today. It is closed from the sea, recorded in the Titchfield Parish Records, and we have a New River/Canal, with a sluice/lock, with contention, and conflicting records, as to when it was built; the sluice in Hill Head Harbour is an obvious, fairly modern, addition. The 3rd Earl had the incentive of requiring the town of Titchfield still to be classed as a port, and to have easier access to the town harbours, and the alternative reasons for closing the estuary have little to commend them, in comparison to the theory outlined above. The closing of the estuary was carried out at the costs of the right honourable the Earle of Southampton and, if the costs of the top and bottom sections of the canal were included in this cost, then the fact that no record of the huge cost of building the complete canal can be found, would be explained; the cost of joining up the top and bottom portions of the canal, maybe in separate sections, would be comparatively small and, therefore, not accurately recorded. The time-scale in carrying out this prodigious task is not known, but it could have taken years to complete and, possibly, modifications and improvements could have been annual events, together with the inevitable maintenance, largely the clearing of debris, dredging the channels and repair of storm damage.

If the 3rd Earl did not use the lake, formed when he closed the estuary, for the passage of ships up to the town of Titchfield, then he is the prime contender for building the complete Canal/New River at, or around, the time that he closed the estuary. The lack of any financial records for such an expensive operation, the need to have the Port of Titchfield in operation, the question of the lack of an Act of Parliament and the failure to establish anyone else who had the incentive, establish this contention. The question of building the new waterway as an irrigation channel is discounted because of the huge cost, the unnecessary size (length and width) and the swampy nature of the meadows to be irrigated. The alternative is that the 3rd Earl, at vast cost, closed the estuary because he could and, some 60 years later, an unknown person, with little incentive, built a canal, also at huge cost, and with no Act of Parliament, which has little credence. In circumstances where there is controversy, it is often sensible to invoke Ockham's Razor: that which is the most logical and simple is usually correct.

Ken Groves

References:
Map (1753).HRO WD331(1614); HRO WD332(1633); HRO 19M48137, Survey; 21M52

MARY BROWNE, 2ND COUNTESS OF SOUTHAMPTON

The fascinating Mary Browne was a twin and she loved her brother for the rest of his life, until he died in 1592 just before their father. The arranged marriage of this budding beauty to the 20 year old Henry Wriothesley, the 2nd Earl of Southampton, was organised by two formidable individuals, Jane, the Dowager Countess of Southampton and Mary's father Anthony, Viscount Montague; one, desperately desiring to add an aristocratic connection to the Wriothesley family, so lacking in any such credential, and the other, a lowly Viscount, wishing for his daughter to become a Countess.

Mary Browne

Mary, only thirteen, lived to bitterly regret this espousal, as her husband soon began to show signs of insanity, and the relationship ended with total banishment and his determination to forbid access to her beloved children, Maria and Henry (the 3rd Earl). Fortunately, for Mary, the 2nd Earl died in 1581, probably of a consumptive disease, exacerbated by his incarceration in the Tower for over-zealously, but inactively, due to his innate indecisiveness, supporting the Catholic cause. Her father, the redoubtable Viscount Montague, arranged the overturning of the cruelly repressive will of her demented husband and Mary, now the Dowager Countess, became the successful custodian of the Wriothesley Estates, and Titchfield in particular, until her son, only 8 years old, became of age to undertake his hereditary right. During those years William Shakespeare is thought to have visited her family home, Place House in Titchfield. It was 13 years before Mary Browne married again; this time to a much older man, Sir Thomas Heneage, a favourite of the Queen. He lasted not many months before departing this world, and it was another 4 years before she married her third husband, Sir William Hervey, who was considerably younger than herself, and was a colleague of her son during the military and naval escapades to the Cadiz, Azores and Ireland during the late 1590s. It is open to speculation regarding her amorous activities between her first and second marriages, but it is unlikely that a woman so attractive could have been devoid of admirers. She died early in the reign of James I, aged 55, and was undoubtedly missed by her devoted son, who had been the happy recipient of the successful pleas by his mother to save his head in 1599, and for his release from the Tower in 1603. She is said to be buried in the crypt of Titchfield Church, and is thought to be one of the kneeling effigies on the Wriothesley monument.

Ken Groves

Thou art my mother's glass, and she in thee Calls back the lovely April of her prime.

William Shakespeare Sonnet III

ELIZABETH VERNON, 3RD COUNTESS OF SOUTHAMPTON

Henry Wriothesley, the 3rd Earl of Southampton, unlike his father, courted and married the woman he loved and the courtship started in 1595, with the marriage to Elizabeth Vernon taking place in 1598. Elizabeth, born in Shropshire, was a lady in waiting to Queen Elizabeth, facilitated by her relationship to the Devereux family; she was the cousin of Robert the 2nd Earl of Essex, the best friend of her husband-to-be. The length of the courtship was due to the great displeasure that the Queen evinced to the relationship, and the wedding only took place after Elizabeth fell pregnant. Henry returned, swiftly,

Elizabeth Vernon

from a visit to Paris with Robert Cecil, the Queen's Chief Secretary, when he heard of the imminent birth, and married in secret. It did not take long before the Queen discovered the facts and promptly imprisoned Elizabeth in the Fleet prison; it is recorded that she had the best accommodation which was available, and Henry was summoned back from Paris to join her in the Fleet. During the rest of Elizabeth's reign they were banned from Court and, of course, Henry was incarcerated in the Tower for his part in the Essex Rebellion. On the accession of James I, all was forgiven, and they regained their favour at Court. The legitimised first offspring was named Penelope, after Penelope Rich, the beautiful sister of Essex, and she married into the Spencer family. One of Penelope Spencer's sons became the 1st Earl of Sunderland and, it can be claimed, the late Princess Diana is a descendant. Following the release of Henry from the Tower, further children arrived, the first being James, named after the King, followed by Thomas, who became the 4th Earl, and two daughters, Anne and Elizabeth. The apparently happily married couple enjoyed twenty-six years of bliss, with Elizabeth helping her husband to reorganise the Wriothesley Estates, spending considerable time at Titchfield on the projects undertaken by the Earl. Disaster came in 1624, however, when both Henry and James, within several days of each other succumbed to a fever, whilst on campaign in the Netherlands; James preceded his father and therefore was never the next Earl of Southampton. The devastated Elizabeth, aged 52, was left to sort out the affairs of the family, which proved difficult, as Henry did not leave a will. The new King, Charles I, came to visit during 1624, and Elizabeth became very friendly with Queen Henrietta, a friendship which lasted for years, until Henrietta was banished after the execution of the King. Thomas, the new Earl of Southampton, aged 17, then proceeded to spend 5 years abroad, leaving his mother to manage the estates with her usual aplomb. Elizabeth, the Dowager Countess of Southampton, continued to help her son until 1655, when she died at the then, extraordinary, age of 83.

Ken Groves

HENRY TIMBERLAKE

One of the most colourful characters in the long history of Titchfield was Henry Timberlake, the Elizabethan merchant adventurer, who retired to Titchfield after an amazing life of international commerce and travel. A journal of his expedition to the Holy Land was transcribed from his letters and published by Thomas Archer in 1603 and later by Crouch in 1699. Dr Joan Taylor has written a book about him called *The Englishman, the Moor and the Holy City* and gave a lecture to Titchfield History Society under the same title in November 2007; this abridged account draws heavily upon these two sources.

Henry Timberlake's date of birth is not recorded but, by 1600, he was a rich, established merchant adventurer who had built a ship, the *Trojan*, which at about 300 tons and with a crew of 60 was a large ship for the period. He lived, at that time, with his wife Margaret in the parish of All Hallows Barking where the baptisms and, in some cases, burials of several children were recorded.

He was established in a two-way trade between London and the White Sea under the auspices of the *Russia Company* bringing back furs, tallow, etc., then sailing to the Mediterranean under the auspices of the *Levant Company* with woollen goods, lead and tin, returning to London with spices, drugs, currants and wine. He had completed a similar voyage in 1597.

Having returned from a successful trip to the White Sea in 1599, he had to wait in London until a problem regarding the Queen's Charter to the *Levant Company* was resolved; he was shipping not only his own goods but those of other merchants in the company. Although he would normally expect to leave in June, it was not until after a new charter was issued on 31 December 1600 that he was able to leave, thus making it unlikely that he would get his woollen goods to Egypt before the weather there started to warm up.

Voyages to the Mediterranean were fraught with dangers at this time; shipwrecks and piracy were common, with captive crews and passengers being taken to the Ottoman Empire as white slaves. The common tongue used by seamen and traders in the region was the *lingua franca*, a mixture of predominantly Italian with Provençal French, Spanish, Portuguese, Greek, Turkish and Arabic.

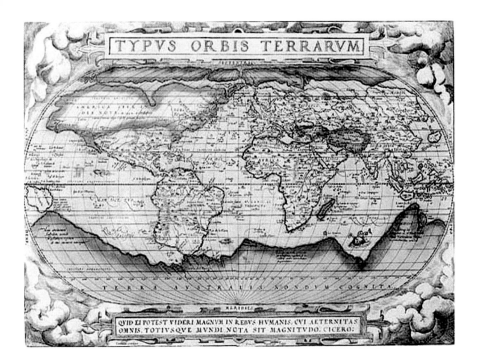

Henry Timberlake sailed directly to Algiers, through the Straits of Gibraltar, having given France and Spain a wide berth. Although Algiers was a centre for the Corsairs, ships connected with the *Levant Company* went unmolested, since England was regarded as an ally of Morocco through a common enmity with Spain. At Algiers he took aboard 300 passengers, Christians, Jews and Moslems making the *hajj* to Mecca. Although he continually had an eye for commerce, he was clearly a fair and kindly man who was well liked and respected by all, including his passengers.

They continued by way of Tunis to Alexandria where the *Trojan* was berthed and disembarked its passengers and cargo. Timberlake, with his assistant Waldred and guarded by a party of *janissaries* conveyed the goods overland to the Nile and thence, by flat-bottomed barges to Cairo, the most important city of the Ottoman Empire. At Cairo he was able to hand over the *Levant Company's* goods but still had to sell his own, and the market for woollen goods had disappeared with the warmer weather. During his enforced stay to seek markets for his goods he met a traveller, John Burrell, who was set on visiting Jerusalem, at the Consul's house. Timberlake decided to leave the sale of his goods in the hands of Waldred and accompany John Burrell.

They set off on horseback and met up with a caravan of 750 camels along the northern edge of the Sinai desert. They were attacked by Bedouin tribesmen one night but fought them off with some losses of people and goods, John Burrell only just escaping with his life. They travelled via Gaza and Hebron to Mamre where Abraham had allegedly entertained angels beneath an ilex tree. Unknown to Timberlake, another traveller with the caravan was one of the Moslem pilgrims who had travelled on his ship from Algiers. He remained unnamed in Timberlake's account but will be referred to as al-Fessi, the man from Fes. One morning, when Timberlake was washing his "fowle lynninge" at a spring he was amazed to be approached by a strange Moor and addressed by name in the *lingua franca*. Al-Fessi insisted that he would do the washing and in future look after Timberlake as thanks for the way he had been treated on the *Trojan*.

Timberlake and Burrell, along with al-Fessi, left with a group of pilgrims who were bound for Jerusalem. Individuals wishing to visit Jerusalem required letters of introduction but Timberlake had none. He thought it sufficient to state that he was an Englishman operating under a charter from Elizabeth I; the guards were unaware of the existence of England or its queen and threw him into jail, considering him to be either mad or a spy! There were no ambassador, consul or other English merchants to appeal to for help but al-Fessi interceded on his behalf with the Pasha, explaining Timberlake's role in aiding Moslems making the *hajj* and pleading for his release; this was granted on the condition that he resided at the Franciscan Monastery of San Salvatore. He was able to tour Jerusalem, sketch maps and note the defences and concluded that it would be very easy to capture the city. During this stay, he foolishly drank at the Pool of Siloam and became very sick; he was nursed by the friars and his attitude to Roman Catholicism softened. He toured extensively: to Bethlehem, bathed in the River Jordan and visited the Dead Sea. His return to the monastery is recorded in its archives.

John Burrell left to return to Cairo, meeting up with other Englishmen fleeing the plague in Aleppo. Timberlake and al-Fessi decided to return alone on racing camels and in the Sinai Desert they were temporarily isolated when one of the camels escaped and their accompanying Bedouins went off to retrieve it. They were approached by a marauding band of Bedouins and al-Fessi saved Timberlake's life by refusing to hand him over to them. When the other Bedouins returned with the camels they vouched for him and they were entertained at the Bedouin camp. When they eventually returned to Cairo, Timberlake furnished al-Fessi with all that he required for the *hajj* and they separated. Waldred had managed to sell all the goods and had returned to Alexandria and Timberlake followed. It was from Alexandria that he sent the letter that became the basis of the published chronicle. The *Trojan* went to Tripoli where Timberlake met up with John Sanderson. The crew were then arrested for stealing soap and only freed after the intervention of *Levant Company* merchants from Aleppo. The *Trojan* sailed from Tripoli, only to be lost in a storm. John Sanderson left on another ship while Timberlake returned to Alexandria where he received the news that al-Fessi had died on the *hajj*.

Henry Timberlake eventually returned to London in 1604 and All Hallows Barking Register records the baptism of another child. Timberlake became involved in a company searching for the North West Passage to the Pacific and in the *Virginia Company* through which he met the 3rd Earl of Southampton. By 1620 he was resident at Chilling Manor in the Parish of Titchfield.

He became a leading resident of the village, being given Power of Attorney by the 3rd Earl for a time. Of the Trustees appointed by the 3rd Earl in the original Earl of Southampton's Trust of 1620, the first three listed were Arthur Bromfield, Esq., Henry Timberlake, Gent. and Timothy Blere, identified as a "clerke". The Titchfield Parish Register for xxv February 1623 records the burial of "Mris Elizabeth Blier the wife of Tymothie Blier Vicar of Titchfield" and, only a few weeks later, on xvi April, it records the marriage of "Mr Tymothy Blier vicar and Mris Sara Timberlake".

The Titchfield Parish Register entry for September 1625 records the burial of "Henry Timberlake gent' the great Traviller in the Chancell of Titchfield the xith day", an honour only conferred upon the most important citizens of the parish. His will is in the Guildhall Library, London and shows that he owned land in Virginia, Bermuda, Essex and London. Among the bequests is one to his "loving friends Arthur Bromfield and his wife" At his death he was "indebted unto diverse persons in diverse great somes of money" and the payment of these debts was guaranteed by Arthur Bromfield.

These affairs show that Henry Timberlake had developed a close personal relationship with the leading families of Titchfield rather than one simply based on business.

John Michell

HENRIETTA MARIA AND CHARLES II IN TITCHFIELD

Queen Henrietta Maria, through the influence she had on her husband King Charles II, was a party to arguably the most significant event in post-mediæval England, the Civil War.

She was born in the Louvre Palace in November 1609, the sixth child of the great King Henry IV of France and his consort Marie de Medici. Her father died while she was still an infant and she was reared as a Roman Catholic. She was a vivacious and lively child and spent her early years in the beautiful surroundings of the Louvre, the Orangery at the Tuileries Palace, the Fontainbleau Forest and the terraces of St Germain and St Cloud. Her mother had planned that all her daughters should become queens.

In 1623 two young Englishmen, Charles Stuart, Prince of Wales and George Villiers, Duke of Buckingham, went to Paris on their way to Spain to woo the Spanish Infanta. They were travelling incognito as "John and Tom Smith" and one of the sights they went out to see was the Queen Mother dining. They also observed the rehearsal of a masque by the ladies of the court. One of the dancers was thirteen year old Henrietta Maria. It does not appear to have been love at first sight, but Charles Stuart had seen, for the first time, the woman destined to be his queen.

Charles became king in 1625. At his accession he was 24 years old and known for his gravity and dignity. He had not been born heir but his older brother Henry had died suddenly before he became king. Charles was shy and reserved with a speech impediment that made him a man of few words.

He had a profound respect for his position and as a king, considered himself responsible only to God. He believed that the monarch's prerogative could not be removed by human means. He was a man of taste and there was no vulgarity about him but, unfortunately, he was infatuated by and under the influence of the Duke of Buckingham; a man who was hated by the Commons.

Charles and Henrietta were married by proxy on 11th May 1625 with the Duc de Chevreuse deputising for the absent bridegroom. The marriage was witnessed by Colonel Sir George Goring who then hurried to England with the news. A few weeks later Henrietta Maria left for England and she and Charles were married in the Great Hall of St Augustine in Canterbury on 13th June. From early in the marriage, Charles took a dislike to his wife's train of priests and women. Charles bride was described by Sir Tobie Matthew as a sweet lovely creature with eyes that sparkled. She was full of wit and not afraid of her own shadow; she could dance and sing exquisitely. After the ceremony there were several weeks of bustle, dispute, continual entertainments and banquets. Despite instructions for the preparation of chapels for the use of the Roman Catholic queen, these were not ready and so services had to be attended in her apartments.

As there had been an outbreak of plague in the City of London the queen was unable to meet, familiarise herself with and make herself agreeable to eminent citizens. In fact, she scowled at loyal subjects pressing to watch her and gave precedence to her French attendants.

In the historic tradition of a progress to several parts of their kingdom, Charles took his bride on a tour of southern England, staying at Hampton Court, Nonesuch Palace, Woodstock and Oxford. One visit was to the Earl of Southampton's splendid mansion of Place House at Titchfield. The visit was reported in the Titchfield Parish Record of August 1625: "King Charles and Queene Mary came to Titchfield place the XXth day this month and the Queene stayed there five weekes and three dayes". From here, Charles went hunting in the New Forest. Meanwhile the discontent and resentment felt towards the queen was further fuelled by events at Place House.

It was reported that on one occasion at Place House there had been an altercation between a Protestant chaplain and her majesty's confessor over saying grace before meals. On another day the queen and her ladies twice promenaded through a Protestant service being held in the hall, laughing loudly and talking.

During the first three years of marriage the couple quarrelled frequently. Charles spoke and wrote of his wife's shortcomings, while she contradicted him in public and made unpleasant comments on English customs. It was clear that they were not happy with their situation. One of Henrietta Maria's attendants, her governess Madame Jeanne de St George, known affectionately as Mamie, inflamed the situation. For example, on one occasion when coaches came to carry the court to Canterbury, Mamie insisted on occupying a seat with the

The Square Tower, Portsmouth

king and his wife and, after much arguing, Charles coldly gave way. From then on, Charles was determined to send the attendants back to France for he felt that they had given their mistress bad counsel and encouraged neglect of her duty to her husband and his country. It appears that, when they left, many of the queen's gowns and jewels left too!

Then, on 19th August 1628, the Duke of Buckingham was murdered in Portsmouth. A shocked and horrified Charles turned to his queen for comfort. Until then any efforts she had made to please her consort had been prompted by self interest but she appears to have been stirred by his devastation. It soon became apparent that the king was falling in love with his wife and she shortly became pregnant. For the rest of their life together they appear to have lived in harmony and unity. They went on to have eight children, among them two future monarchs Charles II and James II.

Throughout his reign, Charles and his Parliament had been at odds but the situation eventually deteriorated into the Civil War in 1642, with fighting between Royalist supporters and Parliamentarians. During the conflict the queen maintained the position that Charles should make no concessions and for seven years bloody battles raged. The Parliamentarians finally prevailed and Charles was imprisoned at Hampton Court.

He was briefly at Place House again after his escape attempt in November

1647. This was his last night of liberty. He was making plans to take ship for the Continent if he failed to obtain satisfactory assurances of support which he anticipated from the Governor of the Isle of Wight, Colonel Hammond, but an embargo had been placed on all southern port shipping as soon as his escape was known at Westminster. An embarrassed Colonel Hammond, who wished to show his loyalty to the new regime, crossed the Solent and escorted Charles with his three attendants to imprisonment in Carisbrooke Castle. From thence he eventually travelled to London for his trial. In January 1649 he was beheaded outside the Banqueting House in Whitehall.

The princes Charles, Prince of Wales and James, Duke of York and Queen Henrietta Maria had earlier left England when it began to look doubtful that the Royalists could win. She stayed in France where her nephew was King Louis XIV. Prince Henry and Princess Elizabeth were moved to Carisbrooke in August 1650 and were treated with respect and consideration, yet Princess Elizabeth, who was a fourteen year old child suffering from rickets, died of pneumonia in September 1650. She lies buried in Newport Parish Church. Henry was released to join his mother in France in 1653.

In 1660 her son Charles was restored to the throne of England and she lived in both England and France during the remainder of her life. She died on 21st August 1667 at the Chateau of St Colombes near Paris and was buried in the Cathedral of St Denis, the burial church of many of France's kings, beside her father Henry IV.

Annie Mitchell

Sources used:

Titchfield Parish Register 1589 – 1634

Henrietta Maria by Carola Oman

Tudor and Stuart Britain 1471 – 1714 by Roger Lockyer

TITCHFIELD TOWN

Next on the Village cast your eyes, where high
In Air the lofty Maypole rears its Head,
And to the World a shameful Peace proclaims:
Then view the empty Market, how the Place
For that erected stands unoccupy'd;

From Titchfield: A Poetical Essay by John Missing, 1949.
Original wood engraving by Anne Tout

ONE THOMAS OR TWO?

The little church of St Edmunds, King and Martyr, with its origins in 9th century, is now a daughter church in the parish of Holy Rood in Stubbington. However prior to 1871, it was part of the Titchfield parish and known as the Chapel of St. Edmund. When Thomas Missing's life was commemorated by a memorial therefore in the 18th century, St Edmunds was administered by the Vicar of Titchfield.

The splendid memorial to Thomas Missing in the south transept carries the following inscription:

Underneath are deposited
Thomas Missing
Late of Stubington in the County of Southampton Esqre
Who was born the 10th day of February 1675.
And died the 6th day of July 1733
A Gentleman much regretted at his Death
Because much beloved in his Life.
As a Private Man
He was assiduous in the Offices of Humanity:
In those of Justice as a Magistrate
In those of Publick Spirit as a Senator:
An honourable Employment acquired by his Merits
He Possessed with Esteem,
Because he discharged it with Integrity.
Nor was a large Fortune
Acquired by his honest Abilities
Attended with Envy,
Since it was acquired without Baseness or Blemish
And employed in acts of Benevolence.
To the honest and diligent he was a sure Patron and Friend
To the Idle and Vitious Severe without Cruelty;
A warm Champion for Publick Liberty,
And for the pure Religion of Peace and Truth;
An Adversary to all Bigotry and Pious Folly
As dishonouring the great Creator and pernicious to ye Creation.
Piety towards God he knew
To be ever accompanied with tenderness towards Men
Whilst Imposture delighted in Rage and Terrors
Such was the Character such the Sentiments and Religion
Of Mr. Missing, Dearest to those who knew him most,
And like him loved Virtue best.Reader
Applaud and Imitate

Anon

It is not known who built or paid for the memorial, nor who wrote the inscription - or even if the memorial is in its original position. There is no mention of its construction in the Titchfield Parish Vestry books in the Hampshire Record Office at Winchester. Thomas, the subject of the eulogy, sounds a splendid, upstanding and god-fearing citizen, who would have been widely known and respected in the village. But who was he? Who were his family? Why, in *Titchfield, a Place in History*, did Trevor Cox refer to him as an agent for the navy? Did he have a wife and children and how did he acquire his fortune? I thought that some at least of this information would be provided by the Titchfield Parish Registers.

The Thomas Memorial

The relevant Parish Register (where the records for baptisms, marriages and burials for both churches were noted) records the baptism of a Thomas Missing on 10.02.1675, the date of Thomas' birth on the memorial. This child was the third son born to John and Ann Missing of Stubbington. I had expected that there would have been many further entries of this family. However there were just two; Thomas was listed as a god-father to a Michael Lunn in 1731 and his burial was recorded as 6. 07. 1733. This date coincides with the date of death on the monument. But how strange that there was no record of the burial of his parents or his siblings, his marriage or the baptism of children. Did the child Thomas grew up in Titchfield? If so, his family disappeared, he remained unmarried, did good works in the community, became a god-father and died. Or was there was something more?

Further searches revealed a Will of a Thomas Missing of Stubbington, proved on 20th July,1733, just thirteen days after the death of Thomas of the monument. Although there is no date of birth or death on the Will, there are a number of similarities between the "two" Thomas'. They lived during the same period, their names match, they are both described as "of Stubbington" and they both appeared to be wealthy, philanthropic gentlemen. The problem of the match however lies with personal details contained in the Will. This Thomas had a sister Mary, a wife named Rebecca and six children, five daughters and a son named Thomas. Why were the births of a sister and the birth of his six own children not found in the Titchfield register? Thomas of the Will lived mainly in Portsmouth although he owned a house in Stubbington. Two of his daughters were married in Titchfield Church and these *are* recorded in the Parish Register. If the "two" Thomas' are one and the same, the fact that his marriage is not recorded is not significant, but the fact that his sister's birth and the birth of all his children are absent creates a real obstacle to matching the two.

Thomas Missing

There is some evidence which would support the suggestion that the two Thomas' were indeed the same. Thomas' parents, John and Ann Missing of Stubbington, could have left Titchfield shortly after Thomas' birth and moved to - for instance - Fareham, where Mary was born. Thomas married Rebecca. They produced two daughters. Then Thomas and Rebecca and the two girls moved to Portsmouth, where three more daughters and a son were born. The baptisms of these last four named children are indeed recorded at St Thomas' Church, Portsea in the Portsmouth registers.

114

Again, further research at the Hampshire Record Office in *Manorial Records of Crofton Manor* lists a Thomas Missing as Copyholder from 1702 – 1729. In these listings, Thomas' death is noted as 1733, which fits the information on the monument. So this Thomas would appear to fit in. Further,he would have been well placed to acquire timber and other materials for trade. He might well have made his money therefore as a contractor for the navy, a highly lucrative activity.

More research is needed to match the two Thomas'. There are still discrepancies in the stories. There were definitely many branches of the Missing family in the 18th century, living in Titchfield, Stubbington, Crofton and Hook, so there is a very real likelihood of family members becoming confused. However, it seems too much of a coincidence that two wealthy and influential gentleman of the same name lived at the same time with such strong links to the same parish. Perhaps it is all just evidence of the mobility of individuals and families in the area, in the 17th and 18th centuries.

Julia R Mills

Titchfield: A Place in History ed. R. Wade and G. Watts 1989*Titchfield Parish Registers 1634-1678* ed. K. Hayward

Family Search Google

Manorial Records, Crofton Manor 1691 Hampshire Record Office Ref no. 36M83/52

A TRAGIC ROMANCE

Now to the Place they came, when lo behind
Out rush'd the Ruffians on the fearless Youth;
They seized him fast, and lifted high in Air
Their treach'rous Blades; the Virgin shriek'd Aloud;

From by John Missing's poem
Original wood engraving by Anne Tout

THE COACH AND HORSES PUBLIC HOUSE
(Written in 2010 before redevelopment)
The former Coach and Horses Public House is situated on the junction of South Street, Bridge Street and Coach Hill, in Titchfield. The frontage of the roadside building is dated from the 1920s, and the building to the rear to this could be some 50 years older. There are other adjoining constructions at the left-hand rear of the site which are considerably older.

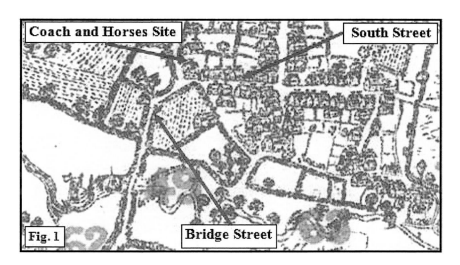

From the map of the Estate of Titchfield, dated 1605/10, it can be seen that the surveyor has shown a building on this site. It has been established that, in all probability, this map is genuine, and that its accuracy is close to that of modern maps. However, this is not proof that there was a building at that site in the early 1600s. See Figure 1.

Another map of the Titchfield Estate was also drawn in 1753, and this shows that there was a property located on the site of the Coach and Horses at this date. Although the map is in very bad condition, the location of buildings shown on this map correlate very closely to those which are present, still, on Ordnance Survey maps. The probability that a building was in existence in the 1750s is, therefore, highly likely.

In the Hampshire Telegraph of March 15th. 1808 there was a report of the sale by Auction of the Coach and Horses Inn, together with the Assembly Room, Arched Vaults, Stabling and Coach House. It can be assumed that they brewed their own

To Brewers and others. Inn and Assembly Room, Titch-field, Hants.

TO be Sold by Auction, on Tuesday, the 15th March, 1808, at eleven o'clock in the forenoon, on the Premises, (unless Disposed of by Private Contract, of which timely notice will be given) All that good accustomed INN, known by the name of the COACH AND HORSES, at Titchfield, with the Assembly-Room, good arched Vaults, Stabling, Coach-House, &c. being a Copy of Inheritance; together with a piece of Freehold Land, adjoining the Street.

The Situation is eligible, and capable of great improvement, being central between Southampton, Portsmouth, and Gosport, in the Western Road; at present in full Trade. Possession may be had at Midsummer next.

A Brewhouse and Malthouse, nearly adjoining, to be Sold by Private Contract.

A good four-wheeled Carriage to be Disposed of.

Apply, for particulars, to R. Gough, Auctioneer, Titch-field.

Fig. 2

beer, because the sale included a nearby Brewhouse and Malthouse. A copy of the Sale particulars are shown in Figure 2.

Just over a year later, in the Hampshire Telegraph on or about 8th. May 1809, there appeared another article, this time advertising the Coach and Horses Inn as being fitted up with a Theatre in the Assembly Room. The advertisement had been taken out by Mr. Adamson, and it is not unreasonable to conclude that it was Mr Adamson, who had purchased the Coach and Horses Inn at the Auction which took place on March 15th. the previous year. There is no date mentioned on this advertisement, but another advertisement, on the same page, describes that there was an auction to be held on 8th. May 1809.

The Coach and Horses advertisement tells us that Mr. Adamson had engaged 'several Performers of acknowledged ability', and they were opening with *She Stoops to Conquer* which, it is fair to assume, is the play written by Oliver Goldsmith, and first performed, in London, in 1773. The audience, according to the advert, will also hear the musical Entertainment of *The Poor Soldier*. This appears to be a comic opera, by John O'Keefe and William Shield, and is described as 'a rather feeble play with a great many engaging songs'. It relates to the return of Irish soldiers from America, where they had been fighting for the British in the War of Independence. For some unaccountable reason, it became extremely popular in the new USA, and is quoted as being the favourite play of George Washington. Both Goldsmith and O'Keefe are Irish, but this does not seem to be relevant here. A copy of the advert is seen in Figure 3.

The Assembly Room and Theatre can be identified from photographs of the Coach and Horses, and it lies on the south-west side of the buildings. It has the appearance of being old enough to be the Theatre of 1809, and the roof, from the exterior, has the characteristics of greater age – maybe 17th century. A structure, adjoining the Assembly Room, is called The Stable and, currently, houses the Skittle Alley. This building, also, shows signs of some age. From a satellite view of the Coach and Horses, the main part of the Public House does not appear to be any older than 100 years.

Figure 4 is a photograph of the Assembly Room / Theatre, with the Stable/ Skittle Alley on the left of the Assembly Room. Cleary, the windows are fairly modern, but the half-hip roof, and the relatively steep roof angle, are indicative of a building which could be several hundred years old, and is not uncommon in the Titchfield vicinity. Figures 5 and 6 illustrate some of the older beams within the interior of the Assembly Room and the Stable, which, obviously, reinforce the suspected age of the buildings.

MR. ADAMSON most respectfully informs the Nobility, Gentry, and Inhabitants of TITCHFIELD and its vicinity, that he has fitted up a THEATRE, in a commodious manner, in the ASSEMBLY ROOM, at the COACH AND HORSES, and engaged several Performers of acknowledged ability, and hopes by a strict attention to the Business of the Drama to merit their patronage and support. The Theatre will Open on Monday, with the Comedy of

SHE STOOPS TO CONQUER!

And the musical Entertainment of The POOR SOLDIER.

Days of Playing, Mondays, Wednesdays, Fridays, and Saturdays. Doors open at half-past six, to begin precisely at Seven.

Fig. 3

Fig. 4

Planning permission has been granted by the local authority, Fareham Borough Council, for the main building to be demolished, and replaced by a series of apartment blocks, covering the whole area of the site, except for car parking space and limited gardens. The Assembly Room and the Stable are to be converted into a suitable dwelling, with minimum changes to the fabric of the building. In particular, there will be no changes to the roof or location of existing ancient woodwork or brickwork. The site has now been redeveloped, preserving the character of the assembly room our first known theatre.

Reference to the Coach and Horses Theatre in *The Georgian Playhouses of Hampshire 1730 – 1830*, by Paul Ranger; 1996 (Hampshire Papers 10, Hampshire County Council)

Fig. 5

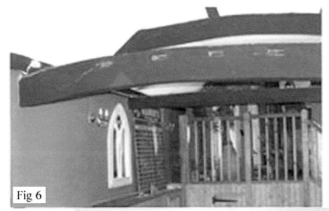

Ken Groves

Fig 6

Fig 7

TITCHFIELD HAVEN WATER MEADOWS

The vast majority of walkers who enjoy the use of the footpath along the eastern side of the *New River* are totally unaware that they are traversing the largest example of landscape archaeology in the parish of Titchfield. Extending over about 100 acres (40 ha) between the footpath and the course of the old River Meon, from north of the "scrapes" at the Titchfield Haven Nature Reserve to Bridge Street in Titchfield are the remains of water meadows.

The reason for this lack of awareness is that, from normal eye level, the characteristic patterns of the water meadows cannot be discerned. Hitherto, it has only been those who have had access to flights in light aircraft or to the results of aerial photography who will have seen the full extent of these works. Nowadays however, the advances in satellite imagery and the availability of the Internet have changed the situation completely. Websites, such as Google Earth, have now made available to everybody access to archaeological survey techniques which have in the past been the sole preserve of the specialist. Recent improvements to the resolution of the coverage of the river valley south of Titchfield enable us to study the water meadows in great detail.

The most southerly set of water meadows viewed from the south (2008)

An oblique aerial view of the same area, from the west.below. The earliest references to water/land management techniques which may represent the origins of the water meadow system go back to the 14th – 15th centuries and

are associated with monastic centres; at Fountains Abbey, Yorkshire, in 1420, weirs were used to flood fields. Monastic houses on the Avon, Test, Itchen, Hamble and Meon are all in areas associated with water meadows but it is probable that the majority were created after the dissolution of the monasteries.

The first clear text on water meadows appears in a book written by an Elizabethan gentleman called Rowland Vaughan about his lands in the Golden Valley of Herefordshire; his claim to have invented water meadows is a matter for debate.

There were three main types of water meadows: floated up systems, catchwork systems and bedwork systems. In floated up systems, hatches or sluices at the lowest point of the area would be operated to cause upstream levels to rise and the water to flood over the surrounding areas. Catchwork systems were used on valley side slopes and consisted of a high level carrier, rather like a mill leat, which could flood over allowing the water to run down the slope into a parallel drainage channel at the foot of the slope. Bedwork systems were installed in flattish flood plains and consisted of intricate intersecting networks of mains, panes and drains which conveyed the water over the surface of the meadows in flowing layers no greater than one inch (25 mm) deep; they were the ones most often used in the river valleys of Hampshire and it is the remains of these systems which are most easily recognisable in the landscape today. The Titchfield Haven water meadows are of the bedworks type.

The man in charge of all aspects of the maintenance and operation of a water meadow system was called the drowner and he was an important man in the community, being paid as much as a shepherd. A good drowner could have grass ready to feed to animals two weeks earlier in the spring than a bad drowner. Well managed water meadows could provide grazing as early as February whereas other fields were not ready for grazing until April or May. Later in the year they gave reliable haycrops, often more than one, and provided lush grazing for cattle in the autumn.

Water meadows were used as part of the "sheep - corn" system where sheep were grazed on the water meadows during March and April, from 10.00 am to 4.00 pm and at night, they were folded on the arable land where their dung could enrich the thin chalk soils of the downland area to yield improved cereal crops. It was said that one acre of water meadows could support 200 couples of sheep (a ewe and her lamb) during the day and they could in turn manure one acre of arable fields overnight. Sheep were not grazed on the water meadows after April because of the problems of liver fluke. The usage of water meadows developed during the late 18th and early 19th centuries as the Napoleonic wars necessitated a greater need for self-sufficiency in food production in the UK and they became part of an integrated form of general agriculture involving sheep, arable, beef and dairy farming. The heartland of water meadows during this period was Wessex – Hampshire, Dorset and Wiltshire but from about 1800 onwards they extended into eastern England, Northumberland and Scotland.

There were frequent conflicts between the various users of the water, for operating mills of various types and for watering the meadows, and fairly complex agreements were drawn up, "irrigation deeds", to ensure that everyone had a fair share of access to the water. In relation to the Titchfield Haven water meadows, a survey of 1740: "A particular of the manors and farms of Titchfield, Abshott, Posbrooke, …"included, under the heading of: "Leases expiring Mich's 1747" several subheadings, including Posbrooke, under which is listed: "John Missing - Titchfield corn mills with the use of the water for watering the meadows…" [1].

With the cessation of hostilities and the development of worldwide trade, the nature of the agricultural system changed. The import of wool and mutton from Australia and New Zealand, cereals and beef from the Americas and the import of fertilisers from South America replacing the need for dung from sheep folded on the arable land, together with a period of bad weather in the 1880s, led to an agricultural depression.

The response to this led farmers to specialise and in Hampshire they turned from the "sheep - corn" system to the integration of water meadows into the more lucrative dairy production. This necessitated just as much work in the maintenance and operation of the water meadows but gave a steady income from milk production throughout the year. However, during the 20th century, the availability of farm labour willing to undertake the often arduous work connected with water meadows and changing practices in the dairy industry led to the final decline of the water meadow system.

Culvert between the *New River* and one set of water meadows.

The Titchfield Haven water meadows consist of nine sets, each being supplied by a large culvert built into the eastern bank of the *New River.* Some of these culverts are intact and only require the replacement of the timber hatch boards to make them serviceable whereas others are in various states of disrepair.

The culverts are brick built of arched construction with an opening about 2 ft (0.6m) wide between retaining walls 10ft (3m) long. The crown of the culvert opening is about 2ft 6ins (0.75m) below the top of the retaining wall and the depth of the opening from soffit to crown is about 3ft (0.9m). On the *New River* side, the culvert opening is framed by vertical, 1ft (0.3m) square brick piers about 2ft 3ins (0.7m) apart. These have vertical chases (grooves) cut into their inner faces to retain wooden hatch boards which could be raised or lowered to open or close the culvert. The water meadows drain at their lower boundaries into the old River Meon.

The date of construction of the Titchfield Haven water meadows is not known. The utilitarian construction of the culverts in brick contrasts strongly with the masonry used for the surrounding walls of the main hatches, or supposed lock, at the Meon Lane bridge which might suggest that they are not contemporary with, but are a later insertion through the east bank of, the *New River*. However, this use of masonry may simply have been to enhance the appearance of what was a highly visible structure. The large culvert at Hill Head, described in the chapter 'The "Old" Sluice at Hill Head Harbour', which was almost certainly contemporary with, or pre-dated the construction of the *New River* is of similar brick arch construction. The recently established date of the mid-1670s for the construction of the *New River* coincides with the development of water meadows elsewhere in Hampshire; at Winnall Moors, north of Winchester, for example. Furthermore, between Titchfield and Wickham the effects of river diversions, by the Lord of the Manor of Wickham, for the operation of water meadows, led in 1716 to a court action brought by the Earls of Portland and Beaufort concerning the interference of the river flow to various mills within the Titchfield estate. A sketch map relating to this action, recently discovered by Penny Daish, contains a note that the river diversion works were said to have been made about 1656 and 1662; the plan refers to the original and the man-made watercourses in this area as *The Old River* and *The New River* respectively.

It may be conjectured that the water meadows south of Titchfield were constructed at the same time as the *The (Titchfield) New River* and that the watercourse was, in turn, constructed principally for the operation of these water meadows.

The interest today in water meadows and their remains comes from many different directions: history, agricultural, landscape and industrial archaeology; leisure and recreation, walking, water sports, shooting and fishing; the conservation of rare wetland habitats, their flora and fauna and the part they play in water table and flood plain management. It is possible to identify many different, and sometimes conflicting, legitimate interests which are as capable today of causing much dissent between various groups as they were between the millers and drowners in past times and it is a challenge to the water managers of today to attempt to formulate policies which will satisfy the majority of demands. In the case of the Titchfield Haven water meadows, they are situated within the area of the County Reserve and are managed for the benefit of nature conservation.

John Mitchell

References

1. Hampshire Record Office 5M53/1110/14

Bibliography

Bettey, J.H. "The development of water meadows in Dorset during the Seventeenth Century". *The Agricultural History Review*, Vol 25, Part I, 1977.

Bettey, Joseph. "The development of water meadows on the Salisbury Avon, 1665 – 1690". *The Agricultural History Review*, Vol 51, Part II, 2003.

Bowie, G.G.S."Watermeadows in Wessex – a Re-evaluation for the Period 1640 – 1850". *The Agricultural History Review*, Vol 35, Part II, 1987.

Clark, M. "The Conservation of Water Meadows Structures", Landscape Planning and Heritage Group, Environment Department, Hampshire County Co.

Cook, H., Stearne, K. and Williamson, T. "The origins of water meadows in England". *The Agricultural History Review*, Vol 51, Part II, 2003.

Cook, H. and Williamson, T. (Eds) *Water Meadows: History, Ecology and Conservation.* Windgather Press Ltd., Cheshire, 2007.

Wykes, I. "Water Meadows in Hampshire". Environment Department, Hampshire County Council.

THE IVES FAMILY

In the chancel of Titchfield Church are monuments to Edward Ives and his son, Edward Otto Ives. Edward Ives was born in Lymington on 9th February 1719 and became a naval surgeon. He served on the "Dragon" in the Mediterranean from 1739-1745 and on the "Yarmouth" in the English Channel

during 1746. He was then employed for a while by the Commissioners for the sick and wounded. From 1753-1757 he served on the "Kent", under Vice-Admiral Watson, and sailed to India. He remained there until his resignation in 1757 and then returned to England overland, arriving in 1759. He acquired property interests at Hordle and also at Titchfield, where he spent his last years, dividing his time apparently between literature and farming. His house was the property now known as Mayburys. He died at Bath on 26th September 1786. In 1773 Edward Ives published an account of his travels: "A voyage from England to India in the year MDCCLIV...also a journey from Persia to England by an unusual route". In this book he shows an awareness of the important work of Dr James Lind of Haslar Hospital on scurvy, the disease now known to be caused by vitamin C deficiency, but which at that time was little understood and which often devastated ships' crews on long voyages. Ives reports having largely avoided the problem on his ship by giving orange or lemon juice daily to the crew in accordance with Lind's recommendations, and that the crews of the other ships, on which this treatment was not available, were very badly affected. Conclusive scientific proof of the value of citrus fruit as an anti-scorbutic came only with the isolation of vitamin C in the early 1930s. However, the circumstantial evidence was too good to be sensibly ignored, and it is a sad commentary on human fallibility (if no worse) that scurvy and its remedy long continued to be a matter of some controversy. Many voyages and expeditions, including Captain Scott's South Polar Expedition, suffered unnecessarily as a result. Edward Ives was a pioneer.

He was married, firstly February 1745 at Rowner to Rebecca Mary Otto Bayer who was buried 27th July 1747 at Alverstoke; secondly by licence 20th June 1751 at Titchfield to Ann Roy (daughter of Richard Roy) who died 8th July 1820 aged 88 and was buried 8th July 1820 at Titchfield. His daughter by his first wife died in infancy. Of his five children by Ann, one son died in infancy, and two further sons and a daughter died in early adulthood. Only his eldest son, Edward Otto, survived to make his way in the world, becoming prominent in the service of the Honourable East India Company.

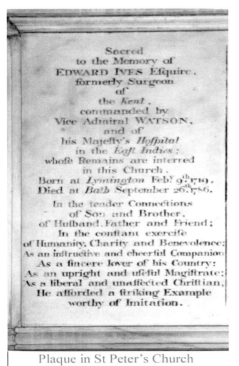

Plaque in St Peter's Church

Edward Otto, born in 1754, was educated at University College Oxford. Having entered the service of the H.E.I.C., he was Resident at Lucknow 1784-1794. He was married in 1784 in Bengal to Arabella Rotton. On their return to England they lived at Titchfield, where he died in 1809. After a short stay on Madeira the family moved to Monmouth, and later to Brecon where Arabella died in 1853. Of their eight children, a son and daughter died in early childhood, and two more sons in their teens. Edward Otto's second daughter Eliza was married in 1817 to John Partridge, an ironmaster in the Forest of Dean, who in 1824 built a mansion at Bishopswood near Ross-on-Wye. They had five children and many remoter descendants. It was she who arranged for the Ives memorial tablets to be erected in Titchfield Church. She died in 1871 and was buried at Bishopswood. In 1873 the mansion was gutted by fire and John Partridge sold up and moved away. He died in 1880 and was buried at Bishopswood.

The second son William Ives was born in 1795 and was educated at Exeter

College and Magdalen Hall Oxford. He appears to have been twice married, having a daughter Williametta Jane by his second wife Jane Rhoda née Lucas. He died in 1838, and Jane died in 1888. Williametta died unmarried in 1916. The fourth son Otto Ives, born in 1801, was an Ensign in the 32nd Regiment and was stationed for some time in the Ionian Islands. In 1824 he was married to Magdalene Diamanti of Paxos. In the early 1830s they emigrated to Ancaster, Canada, stopping in Monmouth for a while on the way. They had four sons, of which more presently. Edward Otto died in 1835 and was buried at Ancaster. Nothing is known of his widow subsequently. The third daughter Arabella Ives, born in 1802, was married in 1824 at Llanhamlach to Rev. Thomas John Powell, Rector of Cantreff and Llanhamlach. He remained there all his life, dying at Cantreff in 1864. She died at Budleigh Salterton in 1886. They had fourteen children, most of whom, however, seem to have died unmarried or relatively young.

Returning to Otto Ives's family, his two elder sons Edward Otto and William Henry were born at Corfu. Both were married; Edward Otto died in 1857 at Milford Haven without issue. William Henry was a naval officer, living near Falmouth. Of William's three children, his elder daughter died unmarried and his son in infancy. His younger daughter Gwendoline Mabel was married in 1917 to Arthur Stanley Williams, and was still alive in 1922. Otto's two younger sons Alfred and Frederick were born at Ancaster. Alfred died in infancy and, of Frederick, nothing further is known: possibly he remained with his mother. Otto's property at Ancaster is rumoured to be haunted. The story is that a local man fell in love with a young relative of Magdalene's who was living with them; on being warned off he committed suicide and has haunted the place ever since.

Once again a once distinguished family has failed in the male line, disappeared into female descendents and scattered.

The earlier history of the family is even more obscure. Edward is known to have had an unmarried sister Gatty, and from references in family wills there is reason to think that he had at least two more sisters, and that there were other relatives in the Fordingbridge, Portsmouth and Gosport areas. Clear proof of such connections, however, is so far lacking.

Keith Hayward

ADMIRAL JOHN BOURMASTER

An insurance company's fire mark on the wall of the Old Surgery at the bottom of Coach Hill has opened up a whole new episode in the history of Titchfield. There may well be other fire marks in the locality which might provide more insight into the past of the area.

Research has shown that in 1781 a John Bourmaster of Titchfield insured a property in Coach Hill known as 'Chawpricks', which is thought to be where the Old Surgery now stands and on which a fire mark (seen right) was attached. He also insured a property in Gosport but this was let to a Joseph Murray, a broker.

There is no known record of John Bourmaster in Titchfield prior to his marriage to Martha Brown by licence on 13th October 1768. At that time he would have been thirty-three years old and be serving as a lieutenant in the Royal

Navy. Martha, who was 21 years of age at the time, was the daughter of James Brown, who, judging by the provisions made in his will of March 1782, was a wealthy local man with land in Titchfield, Warsash, Crofton and elsewhere. Her brother Thomas was to become vicar of Titchfield. The parish records do, however, show that all John and Martha's children were christened in Titchfield some years before he insured the property in Coach Hill and thus all the indications are that John and Martha Bourmaster had settled in the village soon after their marriage.

No. 2 Coach Hill

The Bourmasters had three daughters and a son. Martha, who was born in 1770 and died in 1821, Mary who was born in 1772 and died in 1790 and Harriet, who was born in 1781 and died in 1863. Martha and Mary together with John and Martha's only son, also called John, who died in infancy, were buried with their mother at Titchfield as recorded on the family monument in the churchyard. John Bourmaster is known to have died in Bath on 4th

December 1807 and was interred in a Bath Abbey burial ground, although the precise location is not known and no monument to him has been located.

The Bourmaster's two elder daughters remained unmarried but the youngest daughter, Harriet, married Archibald Collingwood Dickson in Titchfield in 1797 and they had twelve offspring. Harriet died in St. Thomas House, Ryde, in the Isle of Wight and is presumably buried there as her name does not appear on the Bourmaster monument, although the remains of her husband, who became a Baronet and reached the rank of Rear Admiral before his death in 1827, were buried with the other members of the Bourmaster family in Titchfield. The Bourmasters would no doubt have been among many naval families living in the parish and the appearance of Admiral Bourmaster as an executor in the Will of Richard Lee in 1799, in which the members of the Missing and Ives families also appear, points to their involvement in the life of the village.

John Bourmaster's lifetime (1735 - 1807) spanned a period when England was engaged in a number of major conflicts in which the navy had an important role to play and it is, therefore, of interest to examine what is known of John Bourmaster's career in the light of this background.

The young John Bourmaster may have joined the Navy at the time of Bonnie Prince Charlie's rebellion, and may also have served through the Seven Years War, which ended with British success in 1763. Almost immediately, unrest broke out in the American colonies; unrest which led to conflict and, by 1776, to the Declaration of Independence. France and Spain formally joined with the colonists in 1778 in a war which continued until 1783. Then once again there was only a brief period of peace. The French Revolution of 1789 precipitated yet another war in 1793, which with the Revolutionary and Napoleonic Wars continued to 1815. During the period 1740 to 1800 Britain was at war for no less than 30 years and between 1750 and 1800 it has been estimated that the number of ships in the Royal Navy almost trebled.

As a consequence of the unrest in the American colonies, in 1765 it was deemed necessary to despatch a force of 10,000 troops and further regiments followed during the build up of forces prior to and during the War of Independence. These forces had to be self-sufficient and thus had to be supplied by sea with horses, fodder for both horses and men, ammunition and artillery and of course after the capitulation at Yorktown in 1781 the majority had to be brought back home. In his book 'The War for America, 1775 - 1783' Mackesy has commented that the logistical effort required on the oceans during this time had no parallel until the invasion of Europe in 1944. Charnock's Biographia Navalis 1660 -1796 contains no reference to Bourmaster nor does his name appear in the list of British Flag Officers on the active list at the outbreak of war with France in 1793 published in Crowe's 'Royal Navy History 1763 - 1802'. This latter omission is surprising because in 1793 Bourmaster would have been aged 58 and was within a year of being promoted to the rank of Admiral of the Blue, so that one would have expected that, as one of the more experienced officers in the fleet, he would have warranted some mention.

This may in part be because his career falls between 1660 to 1688, when Samuel Pepys produced his listings of Flag Officers and Sea Officers, and 1810, when the Admiralty first began to produce its own official Naval List giving lists of all officers and the naval ships to which they were appointed. During this time the records of the posting of naval officers had been very sketchy. Bourmaster may have joined the navy at 12 years of age or in his early teens, like Nelson and many others did, and he would then have progressed through the rank of Midshipman before being commissioned as a Lieutenant in 1759. His subsequent promotions are found in the Commissioned Sea Officers of the Royal Navy 1660 - 1815 and using a number of other sources it has been possible to prepare the following tentative listing of the ships on which he is thought to have served at different times:

Rank	Date	Posting	
Lieutenant	19 October 1759	1760 Torbay	1761 Valiant
		1761 Portland	1767 Phoenix
Commander	30 May 1776		
Captain	9 September 1777	1778 Defiance	
		1780 Royal George	
		1782 Ocean	
		1786 Elizabeth	
		1791 Barfleur	
		1794 Glory	
Rear Admiral of the Blue	23 October 1794		
Rear Admiral of the Red	1 June 1795		
Vice Admiral of the White	14 February 1799		
Vice Admiral of the Red	1 January 1801		
Admiral of the Blue	23 April 1804		

In the records of the Navy Board and the Board of Admiralty dated October 1761 there is a note stating that Lieutenant Bourmaster had asked to be paid his wages when he was commissioned for the Portland and Valiant after acting as Lieutenant in the Torbay when there had been a vacancy. A later record of October 1769 refers to Lieutenant Bourmaster of the Phoenix submitting 'pay

Glory and Valiant

books and a slop book with three alphabets'. However, by far the more interesting entries relating to John Bourmaster are between March 1774 and June 1775, which give a fascinating insight into the logistical problems in the American War of Independence and his duties at the time.

They start with his assignment to the North American campaign:
1st March 1774

> *"We are to hire transports to carry four Regiments of Foot to different parts of North America and bring others from thence and three Agents will need to be appointed for the service. Recommend the Lieutenants James Dickinson, John Bourmaster and William Cummings....."*

Subsequent entries refer to the activities of these officers; specific to John Bourmaster are the following :-
19th April 1774

> *Lieutenant Bourmaster informs us from the Downs that the Wentworth, Sea Venture and Ocean transports intended to carry four regiments had taken shelter from the wind there"*

21st April 1774

> *"Lieutenant Bourmaster, Agent for Transports, informs us from Spithead that the Wentworth and Ocean arrived there on 20th and the Sea Venture then appeared to be working up. He has informed the C.0. of the 4th Regiment that transports will be ready to receive troops on Saturday morning next and recommend the utmost despatch"*

25th April 1774

"Have ordered Lieutenant Bourmaster to receive the officers tents for the 43" Regiment if they get to Portsmouth before he sails from Spithead if not, shall order them to be shipped on the Countess of Dartinglon, which will sail from Deptford as soon as the tents and equipage are on board"

29th April 1774

"Commissioner Gambier informs us that the transports under the command of Lieutenant Bourmaster sailed from St. Helens yesterday. The officers' tents for the 43 Regiment are now to be put on board the Countess of Darlington...."

So, almost two months after his appointment, John Bourmaster sails from home waters and the next report of him comes from the other side of the Atlantic nearly seven months later - one can only wonder where he had been in the interim:-

11th November 1774

"Lieutenant Bourmaster. Agent for Transports, informs us that due to a shortage of tonnage for the reception of two regiments, his reception for Quebec was changed and orders given to proceed to New York for the 17th companies of the Royal Irish. The transports had about 1500 tons of ordnance stores on board and would be ready to receive the troops and go to sea on October 7th"

12th January 1775

"Lieutenant Bourmaster. Agent for Transports, informs us from Boston that the transports under his direction are employed; the Countess of Darlington at New York for Ordnance stores and flour, the Lively gone to Halifax with Artificers.... the Hunter, serving as a hospital ship for the smallpox, the Empress of Russia and Sea Venture are clearing artillery stores brought down from New York and the Ocean is being repaired for damage received at the wharf in a gale...."

27th June 1775

"....Lieutenant Bourmaster has advised from Boston that the Empress of Russia, Lively and Sea Venture transports were loaded with provisions there. The Countess of Darlington has just returned from New York but was obstructed by rioters and rebels in the city. The Ocean has sailed to Quebec and the Hunter to Halifax to bring oats to the Cavalry expected from England...."

It may not have been necessary for Bourmaster personally to have visited all the locations mentioned in the Navy Board communiqués but he must have been conversant with any navigational hazards in the seaways from Quebec on the St. Lawrence down to New York and possibly further South.

John Bourmaster may have stayed in American waters or the West Indies after acting as Agent for Transports because the Royal George, which had been laid up from 1763 to 1778, and to which he was posted later was dispatched to the American War of Independence after being recommissioned. Bourmaster may well have been on post when the Royal George took part in the Battle of Cap St. Vincent in 1780 before returning home for the birth of his youngest daughter. He was clearly not one of the 900 persons who perished when the Royal George sank in Spithead late in 1782. By then Bourmaster was perhaps posted to the Ocean and may have taken part in the actions that vessel was reported to have fought against the French during 1781 and 1782 before it was paid off in 1783. An entry in the list of Commanding Officers aboard the Victory shows Captain John Bourmaster as being on the muster between the 9th and 18th April 1782; it has, however, been suggested that such a short posting may simply have been a means of keeping an officer on the active list and does not necessarily mean he served on the Victory.

The Barfleur on which Bourmaster served had also been involved in the American War of Independence and later in the French Revolutionary and Napoleonic Wars. Both the Barfleur and Glory took part in the battle of the Glorious First of June 1794 under the command of Admiral Earl Richard Howe. The flag captain of the Barfleur in that engagement was Collingwood so perhaps Bourmaster was serving on the Glory.

After 1794 it is not known whether or not Bourmaster was on active service, In the 17th century the fleet would have been formed in three squadrons, the centre being commanded by the Admiral of the Red, flying a red ensign, the van being commanded by the Vice Admiral of the White and the rear being commanded by the Rear Admiral of the Blue. However, these designations were largely discarded about 1770 and although it would be pleasing to think that his progression to the higher ranks of the navy was earned by merit on active service, it could well be that further advancement for John Bourmaster would have been dependent upon there being a vacancy in the rank above.

In his Last Will and Testament of May 1804 John Bourmaster gave to his son-in-law and daughter, Sir Collingwood Dickson and Lady Harriet, the house which they occupied, the remainder of his estate was to be divided between his widow and his eldest daughter Martha. His widow's will of April 1834 left the residue to the remaining daughter Harriet, after making some monetary provision for her grandchildren.

In the Bath Chronicle of 10th December 1807 Admiral Bourmaster' s name appears amongst other notable deaths of the week but there is no full obituary. The Naval Chronicle of 1807 simply records the death of John Bourmaster, Admiral of the Blue, in his 72" year, with no reference whatever to his service record nor to his achievements and there is no mention of any awards he may have received during his active service.

As John and Martha Bourmaster's only son died in infancy the absence of the family name from the Titchfleld records in subsequent years is not surprising. A Commander Thomas Bourmaster Brown is known to have made his will at Waterlooville in 1840 and the juxtaposition of Bourmaster and Brown may reflect some connection between the families of John and Martha.

In his essay "On a Peal of Bells", the novelist William Thackeray wrote warmly about the Fareham society he had known as a child. His great-grandmother "lived for scores and scores of years in a dear little old Hampshire town inhabited by the wives, widows, daughters of navy captains, admirals, lieutenants. Dear me! Don't I remember Mrs Duval, widow of Admiral Duval and the kind Miss Bookers, one of whom married Captain, now Admiral, Sir Henry Excellent, K.C.B ?" In the 1790s, the Hampshire Pocket Companion, writing about Fareham, described it as a 'place of retreat for many gentlemen of the navy, who support regular Assemblies both here and at Titchfield'. The Bourmasters and the Dicksons show us that there was just such a society in Regency Titchfield.

Donald Green

THE HORNBY FAMILY OF BOMBAY AND HOOK

William Hornby was born around 1723, although his origins have yet to be proved. He was the first of three generations of his name to serve the Honourable East India Company with varying degrees of distinction. When he joined the Company in 1739 as a Writer, John Hornby of St John Street Clerkenwell and Bartholomew Payne of Bishopsgate Street sugar baker stood security for him in the sum of £500. Despite skirmishes with both political and disciplinary troubles he rose to become Governor of Bombay between 1771 and 1784. Like many of his contemporaries, he retired to England as a wealthy 'nabob', with a fortune of £100,000. Perhaps because it was near Portsmouth and Southampton, he bought the old mediaeval manor of Hook near Titchfield, and built a 'nabob house' modelled in part on the Governor's residence at Bombay. It may have been William who built the weir at the mouth of the tidal Hook Lake, turning it into a narrow freshwater lake in his new park. Work began in March 1786 and was completed in April 1790 at a cost of over £12,000. At a further cost of £20,500 he also bought property around Swanwick and in the parishes of Bishops Waltham, Droxford and Wickham. He was married in 1755 in India to Ann Atkins. She died in 1777 aged 37 in North Mymms, Hertfordshire

William Hornby and Daughter Louisa

and was buried there. He was married again in 1788 at St Marylebone to Ann Minshall, who died in 1816 at Portman Square, London. He died in 1803 at Hook House after a severe illness, and was buried at Titchfield.

He and Ann Atkins had nine children, all born in India. John (born in 1755) and William Hunter (born in 1768) both died in infancy. Francis Atkins (born in 1765) was disabled. He was still alive in 1803, but no later reference to him has been found.

Their youngest son Nathaniel (born in 1772) was educated at Harrow and Christ

Church College Oxford. He was appointed Writer in the East India Company, like his father, in 1793. He then held a series of posts, ending as Deputy Paymaster to the troops at Chunar and Commissary of Bazars in 1797. He died unmarried in 1800.

Ann Atkins (born in 1756) was married in 1802 to John Haring of Harley Street, St Marylebone, but was separated from him by 1817 when he was living in Vienna. She died without issue around 1826, by which time he was also dead.

Hannah (born in 1757) was married in 1781 at North Mymms, where her mother had died, to Thomas Holmes of Marylebone, who later assumed the name Hunter, and by whom she had several children.

Elizabeth (born in 1767) was married in 1786 at Marylebone Church to James Law of Portland Place, Marylebone and Canon Hill, Berkshire. He died in 1807 and she died in 1850. They had no issue.

Louisa (born in 1770) was married in 1789 to George Little of Asnagh, County Longford, and later of Pencraig Court, near Ross, Herefordshire. He died in 1826 aged 59 and was buried at Goodrich. She died in 1834 at Regent Street, London. They had several children and many remoter descendants.

William and Ann's second and eldest surviving son, another John, was born in 1764, and was educated at Harrow and St John's College Cambridge. He too joined the East India Company in 1790 as a Writer in the Presidency of Madras. He served as Assistant under the Accountant and Import Warehouse Keeper until 1793, when he returned to England. He was married in 1794 at Walcot to Jane Wynne of Peniarth, Merioneth. He died in 1832 at Portland Place, Marylebone and was buried at Titchfield. She died in 1846 at Marylebone aged 73 and was buried at Titchfield. How much time John and Jane actually spent at The Hook is unclear: certainly nine of their fourteen children were baptised at Marylebone Church.

John's eldest son William (born in 1797) was educated at St John's College Cambridge. He was married in 1854 to Charlotte Bradshaw. He served in the Navy between 1821 and 1825. As a major landowner he features prominently in the Titchfield Parish Tithe Apportionment and the Inclosure. He died in 1869 and was buried at Titchfield. She died in 1890 at Paddington and was buried at Titchfield. They had no issue.

John's second son John Hunter (born in 1798) was educated at Christ Church College Oxford and became a barrister. He died in 1841 at Marylebone and was buried at Titchfield.

John's third son Nathaniel (born in 1800) joined the East India Company in 1818 and became a writer in the Madras Presidency. He then held several posts, ending as Sub-Collector of Sholapore and Acting Collector of Tannah in 1835. He died in 1835 at Tannah.

John's fourth son Arthur (born in 1805) joined the East India Company in 1822 as a Writer in the Bombay Presidency. He was then appointed to a long series of judicial posts, ending as Assistant Judge of Tannah in 1838. After this he returned home and concentrated on managing and developing his grandfather's estate. He built the new church of St Mary Hook with Warsash in 1870-71, together with a parsonage and the school, all at the south end of Church Road. Hook-with-Warsash became a parish, detached from Titchfield, in 1872. He was married to Esther Dornford Robinson. He had been very ill during the building of the church, and died in 1872 at Marylebone. She died in 1912 in Dublin. They had no issue.

John's fifth son Edward Owen (born in 1811) was educated at Brasenose College Oxford and St John's College Cambridge, and became a barrister. He was married in 1849 to Martha Bown. He died in 1882 at The Hook and was buried at Hook-with-Warsash. She died in 1887 at Holders Hill House, Hendon, and was buried at Hook-with-Warsash. They had no issue.

John's sixth son Thomas Wynn (born in 1814) became a J.P. and was Captain in the 82nd Regiment. He lived at Upham House, Upham, Hampshire. He was married in 1848 to Louisa Sheffield. She died in 1904 at Upham House and was buried at Upham. He died in 1906 at Upham House, and was buried at Upham. Their only child, Julia Jane, was born in 1849, and was married in 1868 to the Hon. Albert Hood. She died in 1906 and was buried at Upham. He died in 1921 at Upham House, and his ashes were interred at Upham. They had issue: among their descendants was Pamela Digby, who at one time was Sir Winston Churchill's daughter-in-law.

John's seventh son Henry Hill (born in 1816) was educated at Harrow and Trinity College Cambridge. He died in 1889 at Marylebone and was buried at Titchfield.

Of John's other children, Ann, Emily, Louisa and Harriet Catherine died unmarried. Jane was married in 1819 at Titchfield to George James Perceval, later 6th Earl of Egmont. She died in 1870, and he died in 1874, without issue. Caroline was married in 1834 at St Marylebone to William O'Bryen Hoare. He died in 1886 at Worthing and was buried at Titchfield. She died in 1891 at Marylebone and was buried at Titchfield. They had three daughters, who all died unmarried.

Elizabeth (born in 1802), was married in 1830 at St Marylebone to Rev Richard Buller, Rector of Lanreath, Cornwall. She died in 1875. He died in 1883. They had several children, and many remoter descendants.

There is an enigma regarding a tenth child attributed to William and Ann Hornby by both Burke (*Landed Gentry of Ireland*) and Cokayne (*Complete Baronetage*): Ann, who was born about 1750. They quote no authority for the information, nor does her mother's name appear. In fact she can hardly have been a daughter of Ann Hornby née Atkins as the latter was only 10 in that year. However, a person known as Ann Hornby certainly existed. The East India Company transcripts of Bombay marriages record her marriages: firstly to Richard Eyer in 1767; secondly in 1770 to James Bond (later 1st Baronet of Coolamber), by whom she had several children. She died in 1809 at Kew aged 59. He died in 1820. She, "Dame Ann Bond", features prominently in William Hornby's will, but their relationship is stated neither there nor in his entry in the death duty register. Neither Ann's baptism nor any marriage for William Hornby earlier than 1755 has been found. The question of whether James Bond might have been related to Winston Churchill therefore remains open ...

Sadly, Hook House caught fire while being renovated in 1903 and was burned to a shell. The ruins were demolished soon afterwards, though some of the extensive domestic buildings survive.

Keith Hayward

SIR HENRY WARDEN STANLEY CHILCOTT

Sir Henry Warden Stanley Chilcott, who preferred to be called Warden was born in London on the 11 March 1871, the son of W. W. Chilcott. He became a property speculator and came to Warsash in 1911 when purchasing virtually all of Hook Park with 1210 acres and 1.25 miles of shoreline. The estate also included the large Georgian property of *Abshot House*, *Great and Little Abshot Farms*, *Solent Court Farm and Nursery*, *Fish House and Grange Farm*.

Sir Warden Chilcott

Later acquisitions included all the land on the western side of Newtown Road, south of a property named *Tideway*, together with the site of the present Warsash Maritime Academy. The riverside and coastal frontage stretched from the property now named *The Grooms* in Newtown Road, to the present Solent Breezes Holiday Development.

Planning permission was obtained to develop Hook Park, where at the time only Grange Farm and a few farmworkers' cottages existed. The only road link between Warsash and Hook Park was the carriageway from St Mary's Church to the Hook House mansion, which had been designed in the Palladian style, but destroyed by fire in 1903.

Warden married Beatrice Frances Baumbach in 1894 with records showing the couple residing in Berkshire in 1901, but there is no evidence that Beatrice ever lived in Warsash, therefore one can only assume they became separated. It is recorded she was living in Brighton in 1937 and 1943.

During the First World War Warden served in the Royal Naval Air Service with the rank of Lt. Commander, and was involved in a Special Foreign mission in 1917. He became a Unionist member of Parliament for Walton in Liverpool during the years 1918 to 1929, and acted as Foreign Political Secretary to the Law Officers of the Crown in 1918 to 1922, and in 1922 received a knighthood from King George V at Buckingham Palace. He later served as the Deputy Lord Lieutenant of Hampshire, and published a book titled *Political Salvation 1930-1932*, which is still available from the British Library.

Sir Warden formed a development company named "The Hampshire Estates" and built his own residence circa 1920 named *The Salterns* now renamed *Admirals House* in Newtown Road, Warsash. This was a mansion with sea views, beautiful gardens and lawns sweeping down to the Hamble River. Stables for his racehorses were built nearby, and in the lower part of the gardens near the river was an large indoor riding area, the head gardener's cottage and a boathouse with a slipway. A substantial concrete pier also stretched well out into the river. Further construction followed in Newtown Road with *Red Tiles, Hook Edge and Rodney's, the Salterns Working Mens Club* and a pair of new cottages. A cottage named *Seaview* was also converted into two staff dwellings. The development continued with a concrete road bridge being built over the lake at the southern end of Newtown Road, which gave access to Hook Park. Several large houses overlooking the sea were built in Hook Park Road, and an 18 hole golf course with a professional's cottage was also constructed.

The former Hook House coach house was converted into a prestigious Golf Clubhouse, and the grass fields to the east of Workman's Lane were utilised as a private airfield, for use by Sir Warden's guests. The golf course boundaries were along the coast from Hook Point to the present Solent Breezes, and inland to Hook Park Road and the Golf House.

Ted Woodford

Sir Warden also maintained and frequently used a home in James Street, London SW1 and owned a castle with a demesne at St Florent in Corsica, where he spent much of his time.

In 1921 Sir Warden purchased a brigantine rigged ship of 176 tons which had been built in 1902 as a training ship for the Bibby Line. During the First World War she was purchased by the government and became a Q or decoy ship and received several different names including *Peggy of London*,

Dargle and finally *Grabbit*. Her service was spent in cruising the North Sea as "bait" for the German submarines. In this capacity she was instrumental in the destruction of one of these craft. The Peggy, on one occasion, opened fire when stopped by a U-Boat, inflicting so much damage to the submarine that it surrendered to an armed trawler. Sir Warden renamed the ship *Dolphin* after

Brigantine Dolphin

she had been lengthened by six feet, redesigned and converted into an auxiliary yacht for her owner's use, with the appearance of a late 18th century Royal Navy sailing frigate. She was moored in the Hamble River, a short row from the hard by the Rising Sun Hotel.

During the summer months the vessel would sail to the Mediterranean with Sir Austen Chamberlain, the British Secretary of State for Foreign Affairs and Ivy his wife as guests. On the 30th September 1926 Sir Austen met the Italian Prime Minister Signor Mussolini on board the Dolphin in Leghorn Harbour in Italy, where discussions took place for several hours regarding international affairs. In 1935 Sir Austen purchased a house named *Red Tiles* in Newtown Road, Warsash

Another guest on these cruises in later years with Sir Warden and the Chamberlains was the Contessa Rosamond di Sant'Elia, the estranged wife of an Italian Count, and daughter of a wealthy English ship owner. The Contessa owned a house in Newtown

Sir Austen Chamberlain

Contessa Rosamond

Road, Warsash named Springfields, now greatly enlarged and situated between Salterns and Red Tiles, although, when visiting Warsash from her London home, she preferred to stay with Sir Warden, who became her intimate friend. The Contessa also owned a large house and estate in Kent. In her journal in April 1935 the Contessa wrote that Chillie, as Sir Warden was known, was mad about politics, his political creed was to maintain justice, cheaper food, less taxation, build houses to provide employment, and his favourite saying *"govern us as little as needs be, but govern us when needs be."* She travelled with him to the Grand National horse races at Aintree in the grandest of style, where his box was one of the best on the course. In her own words she comments that Chillie was very kind and seemed fond of her, he was so good natured and full of kindliness, that she could not help but be devoted to him, and enjoyed every moment with his drive and vitality cheering her up. The Contessa showed great interest in the Hampshire Estates programme and personally assisted with the design of the Golf House in Hook Park. On the 23rd July 1935 the Contessa wrote of the conversion in her journal: "It is made out of the old Hook coach-house, quite near the site of *Hook House* - the old mansion which was destroyed by fire some years ago in 1903, owing to the carelessness of a workman who left his

Great Salterns which became Admirals House

blowlamp alight for the night. The huge doors with rounded tops, designed for the passage of the horse drawn family coaches were removed and replaced with great windows. The large portico

144

with round pillars and the front door in the centre of the building were transferred from the entrance of Hook Grange. We were very proud that this had become one of the most charming golf houses in the South of England.".

Sir Warden purchased Owers Farm in Upham, near Bishops Waltham in Hampshire, where stables were built for his racehorses and for breeding. The Hampshire Estates company appears to have had problems and went into liquidation in 1937. Sir Warden retained his Warsash and London homes and spent most of his time during the early part of the Second World War in London, with the head gardener and his family moving into *The Salterns* as caretakers during the early part of the war.

Sir Warden died on the 8th March 1942 and was buried at Upham Church.

Bibliography:
1. Woodford Bryan. 2006. Warsash and The Hamble River, A History & Guide.
2. Woodford Bryan. 2009. Images of Warsash and the Hamble River, 1790-2009, both Warsash Publishing.

Bryan Woodford

The Golf House formerly Hook House stables

145

SARISBURY COURT

Sarisbury Court used to stand at the end of Holly Hill Lane, beside the Hamble, some half a mile south of Sarisbury Green.

The Titchfield Parish Map of 1803 records that this area was agricultural land owned by the Delme' Family and leased to Edmund Cobb Harry who resided in the farmhouse. In 1831 Lord William Henry Chalmondley purchased most of the land between Sarisbury Green and Warsash and commenced building a mansion beside the existing farmhouse. This mansion, which he called Holly Hill House was located in parkland which ran from the present Crableck Lane to the river Hamble, and bounded by the stream through Holly Hill Woodland Park. The tithe map of 1838 records the presence of the new house, together with Wendleholme, the estate dairy farm beside the river.

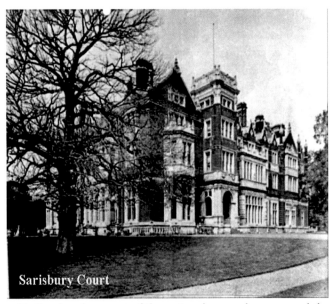

Sarisbury Court

Sir Joseph Paxton (the gardener and architect who designed The Crystal Palace), has been associated with the site, a story commemorated by the name of a local public house. Paxton died in 1865, so it is feasible that he could have been involved with the development of the extensive gardens around the impressive house, together with the landscaping of the parkland which swept down to the river which provided moorings for the yachts.

The estate also included an ice house, now destroyed, and a walled garden beside the stream, where the gardener has been credited with starting the local strawberry industry with his gift of strawberry runners to the local community. However this claim has also been made for the gardeners of Cold East House, and there may be a more general responsibility for the strawberry industry.

Sir William Chalmondley, 3rd Marquis of Chalmondley, was a Member of

Parliament, and significant dignitary in Cheshire, whose family still reside at Chalmondley castle. He remained at Holly Hill House until 1867 when it was sold to Admiral Maxse.

Admiral Maxse was a colourful naval character who had been ADC to Lord Raglan during the Crimea Campaign. His papers are archived as The Maxse Papers in the West Sussex Record Office in Chichester and area, a useful source of information about the site at this period. Many of the records stored (which are so extensive that they require two index books) are associated with the many mortgages raised on parts of the estate, and it is evident that the estate was a drain on resources. It is recorded that Meredith, the poet and native of Portsmouth, was a frequent visitor to Admiral Maxse during this period. Maxse himself seems to have been a larger than life character, well known for his sporting activities and his yacht on the Hamble, and also for expending significant money in attempt to get himself elected to parliament, which he eventually achieved. Maxse sold the estate to Quintin Hogg in August 1879.

Quintin Hogg was a noted philanthropist of the period, and founded the London Ragged School for Destitute Children and London Polytechnic. A tea merchant, he travelled extensively, and used Holly Hill House as a rural outlet for his schools, with all of the advantages of good clean air, country pursuits, and sailing on the Hamble. Unfortunately, his ownership of the estate was plagued by fires, the first in 1879, and the second in 1886. The fire of 1879 took place shortly after Hogg acquired the estate, and whilst this is not documented, the second fire, of 1886, is written up in The Hampshire Chronicle. This records the arrival of 'The Brigade' from Southampton, which took two hours, the need to pump water from a lake, and the fact that Hogg was in India at the time.

Hogg undertook significant improvements to the estate. The house was rebuilt to include an extra dormitory wing, and renamed Sarisbury Court, the river embankment

Figure 2

147

enclosing Bunny Meadows built (or possibly rebuilt), a 'deer leap' created within the park grounds, a coach house built, and the lakes were dug. A second walled garden, which still exists, was constructed beside the Hamble.

Fredrick William Light, who had worked as a gardener's boy for Hogg, records in his Short History of Warsash, that a firm of landscape gardeners was employed to dig the Holly Hill Park lakes shortly after Hogg arrived. This establishes the start of lake construction at about 1880/81. The transfer deed for the subsequent sale of the site shows two narrow lakes, crossed by a central iron bridge. This carried the carriageway which swept down from Sarisbury Court, over a central bridge, and exited by a lodge on Barnes Lane. This lodge still exists as 61 Barnes Lane.

Hogg sold off the estate after the second fire. Sarisbury Court and its immediate park land were sold to Sir Edward Walter in 1886 who rebuilt the damaged section of the house. The lakeland area, including Cawtes Copse was purchased by Montague Henry Foster, and this, together with the surrounding farmland, became detached from the Sarisbury Court estate. The Lakeland area, together with the adjacent Cawtes Copse, was acquired by Fareham Borough Council in 1954 and has been developed into Holly Hill Woodland Park.

Sir Edward Walter, who was the proprietor of The Times, retained Sarisbury Court until 1900 when it was sold to Sir William Garton, who, amongst other things, manufactured HP sauce. The photograph is taken from estate agents literature from 1910 (Fig 1).

Sarisbury Court achieved a notable revival towards the end of World War One, when the American Red Cross purchased the estate to construct what was to be the largest American Army Hospital in Britain, BH40 with a projected capacity of 5,000 beds.

The American Surgeon General purchased Sarisbury Court in 1917, and the American Red Cross was tasked with setting up what

Figure 3

148

was initially to be a 500 bed hospital. The required capacity was soon increased to 1000, and eventually to 3000. This was required to accommodate the 10 per cent casualties which were anticipated in the 'big push' planned for late 1918.

The unit was mobilized in February 1918, and began training at Camp Taylor, Lexington. The medical team lead by Maj. David Barrow team embarked for Great Britain on the 5th of July, split between ships heading for Southampton, Liverpool, and Glasgow, and all arrived at Sarisbury Court by the 30th of July to begin the task of converting the estate to a hospital. This involved building huts and erecting 70 large tents in the grounds to augment the space in the main building, which was adequate for 160 patients and all the nurses. A concrete block making plant was purchased and re assembled on site, timber was felled locally, and a complete laundry was procured in Southampton. The map indicates the extent of the intended development (Fig 2).

BH40, with a staff of 39 officers, 107 nurses, 221 enlisted men and 5 civilians, opened with an intake of 125 patients on the 27th of September 1918. The Red Cross bulletin of the 14th of August reported that it had a capacity for 750 beds, which could easily be increased to 3000, ready for 'the big push'.

The hospital was largely self supporting, and fed with fruit and vegetables from its own grounds, and had a herd of 50 cows, 100 pigs, 1000 chickens and numerous ducks. The armistice in November 1918 made BH 40 largely redundant, though it continued to operate until February 1919, treating wounded and the victims of the devastating influenza outbreak. The photograph is of the Isolation Ward, one of the earliest to be completed (Fig 3).

BH40 finally closed on the 12th of March 1919, with the unit being demobilized in Lexington on the 16th of April. The property was then sold to the British War Department. After a brief period as a retraining centre for returning soldiers, The Court, in a dilapidated condition, was auctioned off in May 1927, and finally demolished in the 1930s.

All that now remains of this magnificent house is a pile of overgrown rubble, though a more thorough investigation reveals the remains of what was presumably the stables, and the quality of construction of these gives some indication of the quality of the main building. The coach house, now extended and renamed 'Inwood', and the gate house also remain as sentinels to a past glory.

The parkland running from the remains of the house to the river Hamble was purchased by Hampshire County Council and is now Wendleholme Nature Reserve. The remainder of the parkland was sold of as individual building plots.

David Redwood

TITCHFIELD'S FIRST BYPASS

Introduction

The construction of the first by-pass is a classic example of one thing leading to another, although there were, in fact, three events - two local, the other national. In 1928 Southampton Corporation promoted a Bill in Parliament to acquire the Northam toll bridge, which crosses the River Itchen, and free the road within the borough of tolls; the crossing became toll-free on 16 May 1929. Hampshire County Council petitioned against this because the Bursledon toll bridge was still privately owned. Both bridges were on a direct route between Southampton and Portsmouth. They reasoned that drivers, having used the toll-free bridge at Northam, would divert to Botley and on to roads unsuitable for heavy traffic thus avoiding the queues and cost of crossing the River Hamble at Bursledon. The Ministry of Transport attached considerable significance to having this important commercial route between the ports toll-free. The county council therefore introduced their own Bill to buy out the owners and tolls on the Bursledon bridge ended on 17 August 1931. The County Surveyor anticipated that freeing these two bridges of tolls would transfer traffic from the Botley - Wickham road and produce a considerable increase on the route through Fareham and Titchfield's "narrow and tortuous streets". Nationally, Britain was facing a time of massive unemployment. Employment in the coal-mining, iron and steel making, and shipbuilding had fallen dramatically between 1920 and 1930. Titchfield, however, was to benefit from this situation.

Ramsay MacDonald's first Labour government came to power in June 1929 and immediately set about creating public works including the building of new roads, funded by the central government, so as to find work for the unemployed from the " distressed areas". Herbert Morrison, the newly appointed Minister of Transport, wrote to county councils asking them to submit road building schemes for which they would receive a substantial grant, providing they used men from areas of mass unemployment. Hampshire's County Surveyor, W. J. Taylor, submitted eleven schemes, one of which was the replacement of the Bursledon Bridge and upgrading its approach roads, another was the building of the Titchfield by-pass. The estimated cost of the latter project was £38000 of which £28500 would be contributed by the Ministry of Transport.

Building the by-pass

(a) The surveys

Titchfield Parish Council's minute book recorded the first mention of a by-pass on 6 December 1929. Mr Carden, the parish clerk, was asked to write to the county council requesting a sketch plan of the route, to which a reply was received that one would be supplied once ground surveys had been made. Mr W Upshall, chairman of the parish council, persuaded fellow councillors that there was an urgent need to write to the Ministry of Transport and the Office of Works to ensure that the new route did not affect the 14th century bridge, known as the Anjou, which crossed the River Meon.

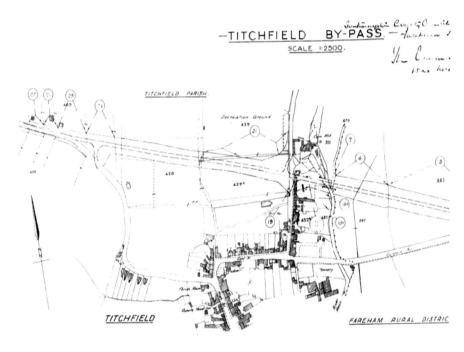

Detailed surveys of the route took place in spring of 1930 and the site was visited by the county Surveyor and various members of the County Roads and Bridges Committee on 25 July.

(b) The Route

In May 1930 the parish council received a copy of the plan, which has not survived, but is described in the minutes of the meeting held on 2 May. "The new road would commence at the top of Titchfield Hill, cross the field owned by Miss Parr, then cross the meadows and River Meon to Mill Street, where several houses would have to be demolished. The road would continue across the allotments and clip off a small piece of the recreation ground at the south-west corner. It would then continue across the first (word unclear) paddock and come out onto the main Southampton road. The road would be 60 feet wide." The meeting agreed to ask that the route be diverted a little to the south to avoid the recreation ground. A year later the parish councillors were informed that the county had agreed £28 compensation for the land taken from the south-west corner and that they would reinstate fences and gravel paths. At a further meeting held on 8 May 1931 the parish councillors agreed that the compensation should be used to provide 10 seats, with concrete ends and wooden slats, and a ladies' lavatory.

The length of the route was about 1430 yards and would require two culverts and a bridge.

(c) Acquisition of land

In November 1930 the County Surveyor notified the County Roads and Bridges Committee that the acquisition of land and cottages might not be completed by 31 March 1931 but that it was possible to begin the junction with the A 27 at the Fareham end of the by-pass. By the end of March the following land had been purchased:-

F. Goodall - £8.19s 0d for agricultural land - HCC to erect post and wire fence and fieldgate – vendor to plant hedge and remove shed.

W. Swatton - £11.10s 0d for agricultural land – HCC to erect post and wire fence, reinstate existing gate - vendor to remove shed.

A. Wells - £3.12s 0d for agricultural land - HCC to erect post and wire fence, plant quick hedge and make entrance - vendor to remove shed.

R. Hill - £9 for agricultural land - HCC to erect fence and gate - £8 paid for loss of crops - vendor to plant hedge.

S. Warn - £7 water meadow, HCC to erect post, wire fence and quickset hedge.

Miss F Walker - £15 pasture - HCC to erect post and wire fence and gates.

The Smallholding and Allotments Sub-committee received £184.19s for agricultural land and allotments, HCC agreeing to plant a quickset hedge, protected by a "Corax" fence, plus two gateways and an approach road.

In April, the county council used the Public Works Facilities Act (1930) to purchase compulsorily the remaining land needed to improve the highway between Portsmouth and Southampton. A map showing the land and buildings to be obtained under the "Southampton County Council (Compulsory Purchase) Order, Titchfield and Fareham parishes 1931" was published but its present whereabouts is unknown. Landowners affected included: Mrs M Foster, J. Nicholson, Miss A. Hewitt, F. Bevis of Waterlooville, Rev. Shaw, E. Wolfe, F. Stubbs of Bishops Waltham for the bed and bank of the river Meon, W. Hudson, the Titchfield Co-op, T. Pinnick, Mrs M. East, R. Williams, Alfred Smith of Segensworth.

Whilst most of the land lost was garden, pasture or arable, the Rev. Shaw received £600 for the loss of some of his garden, lawn and plantation, and the Trustees of Mrs M. Foster £466 for the loss of over three quarters of an acre of pasture, Miss Parr £425, and the largest compensation of £1365 was paid to Frederick Bunney for the purchase of nine cottages and gardens in Mill Street.

These were rented properties and the tenants whose homes were to be demolished were:

No. 4	Albert Munday
No. 5	Frederick Stone
No. 6	Sarah Ballard
No. 7	Frederick Kinch
No. S	Albert Cobb
No, 9	Leonard Wilkins
No. 10	Henry Meads
No. 11	not let
No. 12	Reginald Reeves

Significantly the parish council meeting in November 1930 records that 12 new council houses were to be built in West Street.

(d) Construction of the new road
In March 1931 a tender of £19130 for the groundworks by Messrs John Douglas and Co. of Southampton was accepted by the county council. Fencing the route by labour directly employed by the county surveyor's department commenced in the spring and the contractor, employing South Wales miners, started work on excavating to the required level in August. By November the two culverts had been completed and work would shortly begin on the new bridge across the Meon. However bad weather in the 1931/32 winter combined with 'the troublesome nature of the clay soils' delayed the contactor's progress, but conditions improved during the summer when excavation at the Fareham end had been completed and work had started on the bridge. By November 1932 the cottages in Mill Street had been demolished and the contractor was able to start work on the western part. By March 1933 the contractor had almost finished excavating and back filling the foundations of the entire length of the route. The Fareham end had received a short length of concrete foundation and an asphalt surface and would soon be

open to traffic. Prolonged road works in this section had become a source of irritation to the newly created Fareham Urban District Council, whose clerk had written to the county council in July 1932 about the condition of the by-pass and asking for a completion date. A placating reply agreed that a considerable delay had occurred and that the contractor was being pressed to improve progress. In February 1933 Mr George Powell, an elected member of Fareham UDC, again drew the attention of Hampshire County Council to the great danger and inconvenience to the public at the eastern end of the by-pass caused by the unreasonable delay in completion of the scheme. His motion was seconded by Mr. F Bunney and carried unanimously. By June the excavation, filling, fencing, foundation of the carriageway, drainage, concreting, construction of the bridge over the Meon and the culverts had all been completed. Asphalt surfacing was laid during the late summer and the by-pass opened to traffic on 1 October 1933.

Postscript
A traffic census taken at Park Gate between the 10th and 16th of August 1931 revealed that 3417 cycles. 9968 motor vehicles and 111 horse drawn vehicles, a total of 13496, had passed the census point between the hours of 6 am and 10pm. Whilst other census points around the county had shown increases over the 1928 census, this was a slight reduction which was attributed to the road works at Titchfield and to the closing of the Bursledon Bridge Road to through-traffic, which used the route via Shedfield to reach Southampton. Once the by-pass was open, its value in diverting traffic out of the village is shown by the following figures taken at the census point on the Titchfield by-pass between August 15th and 21st in 1938 ; 37244 vehicles of all types were recorded, an 86.6% increase over the 1935 figures.Finally, it should be recorded that in the autumn of 1934 the by-pass was planted with trees in a scheme devised by the Roads Beautifying Association. Sir Dymoke White donated a number of silver birches in addition to the planned avenue of elms and limes, groups of flowering cherries, hawthorns, horse chestnuts, mountain ash, willows and poplars, which were underplanted by berberis, cistus and double gorse. The passage of time and subsequent road-widenings after the by-pass became part of the A 27 Trunk Road in 1946 has altered the original planting scheme, but in 2009 the route still looked well furnished with mature trees.

Malcolm Walford

Sources::
Titchfield Parish Council Minute Book. Fareham U D C Minute Book.
County Surveyor's Annual Reports. Minutes of the County Road and Bridges Committee.

SARIBURY GREEN IN WARTIME

Allan Cooper was born in Sarisbury Green in 1929. His father Frank was killed in 1942 on H.M.S. Somali, on his fourth Arctic convoy. Allan experienced the 'Home Front' in Sarisbury.

In those days part of the worked-out brickyard was used by Sarisbury and Swanwick Home Guard to practise rifle firing with live ammunition. Once a German aircraft flew low up the Hamble, perhaps hoping to spot the midget submarine that was built at Crableck. Then it turned east following the railway track towards Swanwick Station, machine-gunning as it went. The Home Guard was doing its rifle practice at the time, and they all fell flat on their faces. When they got home, Flo Turner teased her husband: "Charles, if you'd fired straight up in the air, you could have brought the Jerry down!".

Allan Cooper and brother on Sarisbury Green about 1938

In 1943 and 1944 I watched Army Pioneer Corps soldiers build Sarisbury Green D-Day transit camp. Hundreds of British, Canadian and French Canadian troops would be kept in a field and on the Green filled with tents. Paths across it were made with cinders or duckboards. Men threw new uniforms to us over the barbed wire fence: "Lad, you'll find our flashes in the pockets: ask your mum to sew them on for us. Say thanks to the ladies who put the jugs of tea through the barbed wire".

Down Edney Lane I was shown how to crawl under barbed wire tunnels - and then clean some Canadian army boots! In return we were smuggled into a huge marquee on concert nights. The famous Jessie Matthews was one of the entertainers. A camp sergeant spotted us: "What the 'ell are those kids doin' in 'ere. Don't you know there's a war on!". "Sergeant, this boy's dad was killed in the Arctic two years ago!". "Oh, all right, keep you bleedin' 'eads down 'til the Commandant's got in and sat down." One very early day-break I woke up to hear soldiers marching away singing "Paper Doll" and a lewd version of "Roll Me Over". I hoped my Mum wasn't listening.

Regiments came and went - including Irish Hussars, Fife and Forfar Yeomanry, and units of the Canadian 3rd Army. Fraser, whose boots I cleaned, was like a father to me. "When I'm back home to Canada I'll send you a crate of shiny red apples". Word got back that he was killed on the beach. I remember how the Sarisbury Green troops were fed. There were three large Nissen hut cookhouses at the bottom of the Green. I saw dustbins full of dried rice, sacks of potatoes, sides of bacon, and countless cartons of corn flakes.

On my quiet side of the green were ablution sheds and lines of Hessian-curtained latrines. The buckets were lifted over the barbed wire to be emptied into a tanker lorry. The French Canadians got up propped-up duckboards over the barbed wire and ran off with local girls down through Holly Hill Lane to the river. No one in his right mind would have tried to stop French Canadians from getting off the Green. The patrolling sentries were hopelessly outnumbered. "When I was on my landing-craft I could see the little English fields on the Isle of Wight away in the distance. There couldn't be anything better to remember before the balloon went up".

One last memory. My wire-haired white terrier called Pat was fed and put on to a Canadian Sherman tank. Botley police spotted the terrier being held in the open tank turret. They stopped the squadron and seized the dog. His name and address were on the collar tag, and they brought him home to the Green. After that we kept him chained to his kennel, made from tank-shell boxes. I used to play war-time songs on my piano until my mother wept. "Allan, please don't play that again". It was "When the boys are home again all over the world". My parents had made plans for the return of peace. Lots of days on Brownwich shore, fishing from the beach, boiling water for tea on a primus stove. I stood alone at Brownwich in December 2008.

Allan Cooper

THE HURDENS: THREE SONS OF TITCHFIELD

Oscar Oliver Hurden

Our story begins when the parents of our three sons, George Hurden and Anne Hart were married at the parish church at Tarrant Keyneston in Dorset. This was on the 4th of April 1870. The father of the three sons George Hurden was an agricultural labourer on the Charborough Park Estate earning 14 shillings a week. Their first son Willoughby was born on the 5th of October 1876 at Winterbourne Whitchurch in Dorset.

It was in early in 1880 that the family moved to Mill Street in Titchfield where their other two sons and a daughter Fanny were born. Hensley was born on the 7th of August 1882 and Oscar Oliver on the 13th of April 1888. George had secured employment at Titchfield Mill for a wage of 15 shillings a week. He gave all of this to Anne to do as she pleased, on the one condition that she always kept his tobacco jar filled. His pocket money was gained by selling fish in the village, poached from the Meon. The forenames of our three sons may seem unusual in that they were named after the surnames of previous employers of George. The additional name of Oscar for the third son

157

being from Anne's liking for the works of Oscar Wilde.

All three boys attended the Old School in West Street Titchfield. After leaving there each in turn worked as labourers for various landowners in the parish. However each saw that their prospects of a more satisfying career lay in joining the Royal Navy.

Willoughby joined the Navy on the 23rd November 1897 as a Stoker. In 1901 he was in South Africa, and from 1902 to1904 in Somaliland. His ship during this time was H.M.S. Naiad. It was while he was serving in South Africa that he became one of the many Field Gun Crews that relieved the siege on Ladysmith. This is duly recorded on a plaque in St Peter's Church in the village. He was aboard the battleship H.M.S. Revenge at the Battle of Jutland. Willoughby was demobbed from the Royal Navy on the 23rd October 1919. He obtained the position of the Custodian of Titchfield Abbey in the 1920's, looking after the grounds inside the Abbey.

Willoughby married Mary Stapley from Havant in 1923 and in the 1930's they rented a small holding of two and a half acres, which Willoughby named "Revenge" after the ship that he had previously served on at Jutland. This was situated on the right hand side going west up Segensworth Road. The site had a number of wooden farm buildings, one of which he converted into a house. The building had no footings, just a concrete base. This was to be quite fortunate as during a bombing raid on the Southampton to Fareham Railway Line in the Second World War, a bomb landed some 50 feet from the house. The subsequent blast blew the entire building sideways by some two feet, leaving the house intact except for some broken windows. A similar bomb crater of this type can still be seen when taking the train from Fareham to Botley (when the train is between Funtley and Wickham look out on the right hand side at a large open field in the centre of which is the crater). The events of that night were not without some loss of life. A dog from a house across the road was missing the next morning and could not be found. This mystery was solved some five years later when Willoughby decided to trim a boundary hedge with his brother Oscar. During this process the skeleton of a dog was discovered deeply embedded amongst the branches; the missing animal had been hit by the bomb's blast all those years before.

Hensley our second son, joined the Navy on the 5th February 1907 also as a Stoker. He was on board the Battle Cruiser H.M.S. Princess Royal at the Battle of

Jutland at which the ship sustained 9 hits. Hensley was demobbed from the Royal Navy on the 2nd October 1928. He became a market gardener and lived on his small holding in Ranvilles Lane, with his wife Kate Smith from Portsmouth who he had married in 1925. In due course a son George Hensley was born in true naval tradition on Trafalgar Day 21st October 1926.

Oscar Oliver on leaving school became a telegram boy in Titchfield. He joined the Navy in 1906, also as a Stoker, on becoming 18 years of age. His six month shore training was at H.M.S. Nelson; his first draft was to H.M.S. Spanker, which was a torpedo gun boat. His next draft in 1909 was to H.M.S. Indefatigable, later to become H.M.S. Malpomine, a second class cruiser. It was while the ship was visiting the West Indies in 1910 that he saw Halley's Comet. He came home for 108 days shore leave having been informed of his Mother's death on the 9th of June 1911. He was then drafted to H.M.S. Weymouth, a light cruiser, for 10 days steam trials. After this he was drafted to T.B.1 (Torpedo Boat 1) an experimental boat, for six months. He then requested a draft to the Royal Yacht Victoria & Albert, where he remained until the outbreak of the First World War in 1914. It was while he was serving on the Royal Yacht that he married a Portsmouth girl Winifred Cooke on the 12th May 1913. The next three years were spent aboard the battleship H.M.S. Agincourt including its participation in the Battle of Jutland on the 31st May 1916. Oscar's ship was more fortunate than that of his two brothers in that it was undamaged at the end of the engagement. Oscar Oliver had been promoted to Leading Stoker March 1916 and Stoker Petty Officer in 1917. He now served aboard H.M.S. Mallow until the end of the war and the year after, which involved the ship in mine clearance duties caused by the German raider ship "Wolf". By 1920 Oscar Oliver had been drafted back to the Royal Yacht again and by 1930 had been promoted to Chief Petty Officer.

After the death of his first wife Winifred in 1934, Oscar Oliver married Violet Wallace of Fareham on the 13th February 1935. They lived in Gosport Road, Fareham. At the outbreak of the Second World War Oscar Oliver was drafted to H.M.S. Barrage, which was a boom defence vessel until 1942. Then he was drafted to H.MS. Scomber; a Fleetwood Trawler. In 1944 he was drafted to another boom defence vessel H.M.S. Barcroft from where, in 1945, he went to St. George Barracks for demobilization. On leaving the Royal Navy he joined the civilian staff of H.M.S. Collingwood until his retirement at the age of 69 in 1957.

The brothers' lives provide a permanent reminder of the close connections between the parish of Titchfield and the Royal Navy.

Oliver Hurden

In early times the farmers who grew grain also acquired brewing skills and opened the first public beer houses. One of the oldest in Titchfield was the Old Inn House on West Street and it still looks as though it was previously a farm. The early premises were small and informal, offering just a single open room,

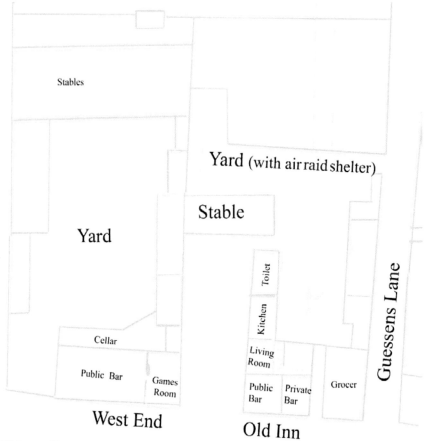

West Street (from old map)

probably catering for the same group of friends and relations each day. There was no bar to lean on and no beer engines; drinks were filled from jugs and tapped from freestanding barrels. Another old beer house was the George, which was the last building by the canal in Bridge Street. It would have been ideally sited for Titchfield sailors, fishermen and barge crews - if indeed there were barges on the canal.

 Our taste for beer became more refined; all kinds of processes and additives were used to vary the flavours, principally by adding different types of hop and malting treatments. As well as ordinary ale, there were best bitters, browns, milds, stouts, pale ales, barley wines and many more. Regional beer companies were founded to offer better quality products and more predictable supplies.

Titchfield's most successful brewery was founded in 1744; it produced a range of products both for sale by the glass and the bottle. Amongst their offerings, Fielders added 'Special Bitter', 'XXXX Brown Ale', 'Dinner Bitter Ale' and 'Family Stout', showing a strong marketing approach. On the 17th November 1806, the Bell Inn, the Horse and Jockey pub and brewhouse, all in New Alresford, were being auctioned on behalf of the Fielders.

The brewing industry would become one of England's major sources of revenue. Larger breweries would evolve and be strictly regulated for the government by HM Customs and Excise in terms of brewing installations, ingredients, alcohol levels and taxable revenue. In a bid to improve the service the beer engine was an innovation to make for a slicker bar service. Designed by a Yorkshire inventor, Joseph Braman in 1797 it drew drinks straight out of the barrel, stored in the 'cellar' to a tap on the bar top via an atmospheric system of pipes and spiles. Quality control and presentation was made possible by the ability to control temperatures and pressures. Clarity and flow of the drinks became ever more important in the pub business.

Another change came in around 1785 when improved roads made stagecoach travel feasible; coaches from Portsmouth to Winchester, Southampton and the Bath - Bristol mail coach were routed through our village. The latter arrived between 7am and 8am and then set out to Bath. In 1831 the Bristol Royal Mail ran through Titchfield, then to Southampton, Salisbury and Beckington near Frome, and Bath. So several village inns began to support the coach trade by supplying horses and regaling the passengers.

Before he Avenue, the way from Fareham was through Catisfield, down Fishers' Hill, over the Meon River by Anjou Bridge (opposite the abbey), left into Mill Street, along East Street and up Southampton Hill. The first inn on this route is the Wheatsheaf and in 1859 Jas Perricott is the licensee; in the years 1872 to 1875,

George Primmer is the next recorded licensee with William Cooper the property owner. By about 1900, Briton G. (Brit) Pearce was in charge and the enterprise had grown considerably. Large doors on Mill Street secured the stables, whilst the three adjoining cottages were the accom[]odation offered in the picture. Brit appears in a number of early carnival photographs; 100 years later proprietor, Adrienne Denoya and her regulars twice won the decorated pub class against stiff competition from the other village pubs in 2003 and 2004. Other inns provided most of the livery horses in High St. and The Square, an extension of High Street. The Queen's Head, a strong survivor

down the years is a handsome double bay-fronted inn that had extensive stables and outbuildings. Early in its function as a coaching inn Jas. Bailey presides, but by 1871 Henry George Broome had taken over. However by 1872 it had joined the Fielder group and John Jennings held the license. Thankfully it has kept its many doors that once departmentalised its business into the lounge and public bars, an off license and the hotel entrance, as was the custom.

The Bugle Hotel wins on size; it was originally a house but was changed into a hotel in 1753, James Brown was the innkeeper and the property belonged to Titchfield manor. Since then it has always been the village focus and logically it was a premises for the Court Baron with Henry Peter Delmé, Lord of the Manor. This imposing building is built on three levels, with large cellars. The third floor rooms are in the roof space; a facade with blank sash windows hides their dormers. Moving around in these attics is a matter of duck or grouse; such are the very low ceilings. In the picture the sign on the left announces all the services that were on offer in the 'Bugle Hotel Mews'. Some of the stables and coach houses are now converted into a single function room.

In the nineteenth century it acquired the building to the south and created the 'Village' bar, but in the twentieth century all three of the front rooms were combined into a single bar.

When the Coach and Horses ended its time as a pub in May 2009, it had been in business for at least 200 years. The old Assembly Room building was once used as a theatre. It is also reported to have been part of an early transport network linked with Gosport and stabled its own horse and carriage. It was rebuilt in 1929 to have a fashionable three bar arrangement and was once the successful venue of the village folk club..

Insert: Bugle Hotel Mews

South Street is still graced by the cozy features of the Red House, another former beer house. The front is typically cottage style but to the rear there are barn doors, stables and a large function room that had a high domed ceiling, giving the impression that it served an active social life. In the years 1830 to 1890 music hall nights, smoking concerts and early movies were popular in public houses. In 1889 the licensee, Charles West sold the products of Hurst & Company, a brewery in

Red House, South Street

The King's Head now Cordwainers

Gosport. Curiously the records show a Richard Lock as both a bricklayer and beer house keeper at the Red House, Titchfield in 1875. Mr. Cave Kingman and family then started their 38 year residence selling the beer of Kinnell & Hartley, a brewery based in Emsworth. In 1921 he revoked the licence and it became a shop, Bandmaster Pure Virginia Cigarettes sponsored livery will be seen in the photograph and in 1946 it was the village post office administered by the postmistress, his daughter, Miss Ruby Kingman.

The King's Head was also on South Street. It had been adapted from two cottages and there was plenty of land at the rear for horses. There is no fancy artwork on the sign outside and one gets the feeling that the Kings Head offered a fairly utilitarian service. In 1859 Alex Whitcher was the proprietor, followed in 1871 by Samuel Brewer. By 1885, Ronald and Ellen Hooper had began their period of tenure.

The Horse & Groom was a public house opposite the Old Inn on West Street that sold United Breweries ales. Elizabeth Bath was the licensee between 1872 and 1875, for William Frederick Feltham, the registered owner. In 1903, Francis Philip le Cornu held the license but one year later Charles Henry Mitchell had taken over. After only six weeks it lost its licence when the police reported drunkenness. Before 1889 the Southampton railway line terminated at Netley Hospital; in that year it was finally extended, linking to Southern Railway to the Fareham and Gosport line. The leather making business opposite the abbey became the Railway Hotel, a hostel for railway workers and went on to host the Welsh miners who built the A27 Titchfield bypass. J R Fielder renamed it the Fisherman's Rest in 1913 with Alfred James Hughes installed as the Licensee. Although the bypass effectively bisected the village and made what was once an important area seem rather remote, the 'Fish' is still popular and is one of the pubs that survives of the fourteen that once served the village.

The Crown was once a pub at 11 Mill Street and there is an adjoining door to number 11 and number 15 bears the sign 'Malt House'. Over the front door there is access to the upper floor via a hoist. To the rear there are the remains of a malting kiln. Connected to this there is evidence of floor where the grain would be dried and malted. Good malt would be needed by the many bakers and brewers in the village in the 18th, 19th and 20th centuries.

Not since the 1920s has the Clarendon quenched the thirsts of the village. Now this three-story, double fronted house (once known as the Corner House) stands in its own orchard at the junction of East Street and High Street. There are signs of stables and most likely a brewery at the rear. What we can see of the early layout suggests that it was in

Numbers 15 to 11 Mill Street

1815 a single room hostelry belonging to Titchfield Manor. We can trace the title of beerhouse keeper through the Collins family to William Moore and his wife Mary Ann Moore, who wrote to Henry Peter Delme' to give notice of their commitment to a franchise contract and when William dies, she continues to run it herself. But the property deeds pass out of the Delme' estate as Andrew Barlow makes the Clarendon the third Titchfield outlet for his beer as his company celebrates its tenth year.

In West Street the front of the West End shows the date 1912. It had a number of small rooms where business could be conducted on a regular basis. One such regular meeting exchanged contracts to supply strawberries to Covent Garden market; the local grower received a hand of bananas to seal an agreement.

This was still a popular pub in the 1980s; never more so than on carnival day where farm folks would gravitate there, leaving West Street blocked with tractors and floats. Engravings on the windows still tell us that like the Old Inn next door it sold Barlows Ales,. although it was in Whitbread hands when it finally closed.

Andrew Barlow's Victoria Brewery in Southampton would have faced stiff competition from three breweries in the village; there was the Hope Brewery on the Titchfield Motors site, another right opposite the Clarendon, and J. R. Fielder in Bridge Street. In later times the Fielders faced a take over bid by the Bethune Leggetts Hope Brewery but in 1881, Fielder turned the tables and acquired the Hope instead. Country wide capitalisation in the 1960s touched our village when John Fielder sold his business to the Whitbread empire.

Titchfield water mill, originally built in about 972 was in 1998 sensitively converted into a licensed restaurant. Many of the mill workings have been preserved in non-working condition and can still be appreciated, whilst the top floor, which you may visit by arrangement, remains untouched.

In 1989, a government bill contrived to reduce the influence of six largest national breweries, by limiting the size of their tied estates. It was reasonably successful in ending regional brand dominance and more guest beers appeared at the pumps. However it caused many of them to reform as new smaller property management companies and sub-contract their brewing operations. In order to grow the size of their estates, they borrowed from the banks using future rental income as collateral, a process known as securitisation. As beer sales continued to decline thus yielding less gross discount from the brewers, rent from lessees has been used to find a greater part of bank repayments. This has also led to under-performing pubs being sold off and many were de-licensed. The last pubs to close in the village were the West End and the Coach & Horses; thankfully this has been balanced by a growth in smaller independent breweries that are able to produce some Cask conditioned real ales that appeal to the connoisseur. At the beginning of 2010, just four public houses remain in the centre of the village, the Wheatsheaf, the Queen's Head, the Fisherman's Rest and the Bugle Hotel; the former three providing food and the latter accommodation, as well.

At its height the pub trade prospered in Titchfield, but now customers face tougher drink-driving laws, high prices in the tied pubs and competition from shops with alcohol licences. Folks now buy their drinks in cans at these shops and sink slowly into their sofas by the telly. There is still however a good choice of beer in Titchfield and some interesting local real ales to sample.

References:
HRO Winchester
Beer & Skittles: Richard Boston, CAMRA

Paul Hawkins

Hampshire Tigers Scout Band leading Titchfield carnival in 1990

TITCHFIELD DOCTORS

We know from parish registers, from inscriptions in the parish church, from Wills and other sources, of at least a dozen surgeons and doctors living in Titchfield before 1858. They included naval surgeons, an apothecary, a surgeon/man-midwife and a barber surgeon. The Royal Navy surgeons had been ships' surgeons who had retired here; the village was lucky to have this group of qualified doctors available before the 1858 Act. There is a fine monumental inscription to one of the doctors, Samuel Croppe, who died in 1710, on the north wall of the chancel of the parish church. In the 1740s, the parish Vestry appointed Thomas Cawte and Richard Lee to visit the parish workhouse in Mill Street. A map of the houses in Titchfield, from about 1840, shows a house designated as The Doctor's House situated on the east side of High Street, close to the Bugle Inn. In 1853 Edward Andrews was surgeon and the Registrar of Births, Marriages and Deaths. All these medical men were, of course, private practitioners, and not publicly supervised.

The situation was altered for good by an Act of Parliament in 1858, instituting a Medical Register to which a doctor was admitted on submitting evidence of adequate training. This meant a degree from a university or Royal College this, effectively excluded charlatans, as the Act disallowed charging fees for medical advice and treatment unless they were on the Register. Shortly after this the Medical Directory was first published as an Annual, and as a commercial venture. It allowed anyone to look up their local doctors, and historians to find out who they were. Unfortunately the early editions have been lost in the various take-overs which have occurred over the years.

The first doctor recorded in the Directory in Titchfield was Dr. Francis Rawle. He became an MRCS in 1864 but had been an LSA since 1844. This is a qualification acceptable for registration, so he may have been here since then. He wrote papers on the treatment of scalp wounds, preservation of Ergot of Rye, and a guide to the Medical Chest Companion, so he was clearly a man of many parts; he had studied at University College London. There is no record of where in the village he lived, but he was in the Directory in 1888 and 1889.

The Old Surgery

The next doctor was William Hoare from 1888 to 1903.He was recorded in 1888 in Hillhead, Titchfield. He gave his qualifications as LRCP& LM(Edinburgh)1872, MRCS (Eng) and LSA 1855 in that order. He was an associate of Kings College and he is a recorded Admiralty surgeon, which suggests where he had spent his time since 1855. During his time the Old Surgery house at 2, Coach Hill was bought from Mr. John Fielder, who had the house and brewery next door. The purchaser at the time was not Dr. Hoare but Mrs Hoare who owned it until it was sold to Dr. Hanson in 1903. It remained as the village surgery until 1977.

Dr. Arthur Stephen Hanson was recorded in Titchfield from 1892 to 1905, He was, presumably, an assistant to Dr Hoare until 1903 when Dr. Hoare died. Dr. Hanson's list of credentials in the directory indicates the way medical practice was going. In 1905 he was recorded as in partnership with Dr. Cade, his successor - the first Partnership in Titchfield.

Dr. Cade, MRCS, LRCP(Lond.) 1888(St Mary's Hospital), Medical Officer and Public Vaccinator, No.1 district, Fareham Union (smallpox compulsory vaccination and workhouse doctor) Surgeon to Foresters and other friendly societies, Medical Officer to Prudential (big even then), House Surgeon and resident Obstetrical Officer to St Mary's Hospital and House Surgeon to Paddington Green Children's Hospital; a good CV even by modern standards. At the time no young doctors had to work in hospitals so Titchfield was indeed lucky. Unfortunately Dr. Cade, the father, died in 1906 leaving his son, Dr. Sidney Cade, who is still remembered in the village, and continued working until 1930. Dr. Sidney Cade's son became a medical student in London Hospital and would likely have succeeded his father. However in 1914 he enlisted in the Royal Hampshire Regiment and was killed at the first battle of the Somme in 1916, a tragedy for the family; he is remembered by the brass plaque on the wall of the north side of St. Peter's Church.

IN PROUD AND LOVING MEMORY OF
FRANCIS THOMAS DARREL CADE,
CAPTAIN 11ᵀᴴ BATTALION HAMPSHIRE REGIMENT, (PIONEERS)
WHO WAS KILLED IN ACTION NEAR CINCHY,
BATTLE OF THE SOMME, FRANCE,
SEPTEMBER 6ᵀᴴ 1916, AGED 21 YEARS,
ONLY SON OF SIDNEY E. P. CADE. L.R.C.P., L.R.C.S., EDIN.,
AND ETHEL, HIS WIFE, OF TITCHFIELD.
HIS LIFE FOR HIS COUNTRY, HIS SOUL TO COD.

Dr. Sidney Cade's time was notable for the Lloyd George Health Act which enabled working men and women to be eligible to take part: it did not cover wives and children, and relied partly on weekly contributions from the members. It covered general medical consultations and treatment such as it was, but not hospital care; it was administered by registered Friendly Societies, of which the largest in Titchfield was the Foresters, who had monthly meetings in the parish rooms, until recently. They were responsible for paying the doctors for the patients on their panel and for collecting their members' contributions. However no one with an income over £400 was allowed to join and they had to pay for care privately, as before. Although the Act was passed in 1911 it was not implemented until 1921 when the first Lloyd George envelopes were issued to doctors for their Panel patients for medical records. These continued in use until the advent of computerisation in the late 1980s, and all the doctors in Titchfield from Dr Cade onwards were involved in this system.

Sidney Cade invited Dr. Windemer to join him in 1924 and, when he retired in 1930, Dr. Windemer took over, continuing through the Second World War, in spite of having serious heart disease. Many more people came following the blitz on Portsmouth; only two doctors were left on the west side of Fareham and both were ill. During this time Dr. Janet Shakespeare was conscripted to come here. She was a Scot and a war widow with one child, so things were difficult for her. She opened a surgery in Park Gate. She was the first woman doctor practising in Titchfield, although patients had to go to Park Gate to see her in surgery.

Dr. Ian Edwards came as an assistant to Dr Windemer in 1946. He graduated through St Mary's Hospital, Paddington and was working at St Mary's Hospital, Portsmouth. There was still no National Health Service and Titchfield was a rough place. Ian Edwards told a story of the first carnival night after the war, when he stitched up patients inside, while Windemer collected half-a-crown from each one.

In 1948 Dr. Windemer retired and sold the practice at 2, Coach Hill to Drs. Edwards and Leslie Ellis. This was the last time the goodwill of a practice was sold in Titchfield as this was made illegal by the National Health Act the next year. By now they were in partnership with Dr. Mackie of Sarisbury Green for night calls and weekend work. Dr. Mackie tragically died in a drowning accident off the Isle of Wight and Dr. Edwards moved to Sarisbury permanently, to fill the gap.

The National Health Service had altered things considerably, the hospitals having been taken over. In addition everyone was entitled to free-at-the-time care and treatment on a Panel basis for Government payment. In Titchfield the National Health Service included the GPs, any dentists and the district nurse/midwife, who was still administered by Hampshire County Council. It was all very difficult for the doctors as they could not assess how many patients they would get and, so, how much work and how much pay. However, Dr Ellis, a

Yorkshireman, had just spent 4 years in a Japanese POW camp and was not fazed by all this, and the two doctors continued alone until 1954 when Dr Rodney Walsh joined them. He worked half the time in

Margaret and Kenneth Dunton

Titchfield with Dr Ellis and half with Dr Edwards in Sarisbury Green.

During the next few years the beginnings of childhood immunisation were undertaken on the practice's own initiative. It started with diptheria and tetanus and was extended over the next 40 years to include polio, whooping cough, German measles, and measles itself. All these were potentially fatal or crippling diseases and were almost eliminated. The international success story was smallpox, which was eliminated so successfully worldwide that it has been possible to stop vaccinating.

Dr. Kenneth Dunton joined Dr. Ellis in 1961 and Dr. Walsh left to work full time in Sarisbury Green. There were new surgeries at Park Gate and Titchfield in 1971 and 1977 respectively, the latter during the Jubilee Fleet review. The designs followed a surgery seen in Toronto, Canada and replaced working in doctors homes; they were unusual for the times.

The work of the doctors began changing more rapidly at this time. Chiefly there were population changes: a much higher proportion of over 80s: and diseases such as diabetes and degenerate arterial and other blood diseases and many others which require prolonged specialist nurse monitoring. Another difference was that pregnant women went to Portsmouth or Southampton hospitals largely because with new methods of monitoring mother and baby it became much safer in hospital. As at one time 30% of births had been home deliveries; this was quite a change for doctors with an interest in the subject.

In 1966 Dr. Margaret Dunton from Manchester University joined the partnership, working from Park Gate, followed by Dr. Elspeth Taylor from Liverpool University in 1968. They were the first of an increasing stream of women graduates who altered the practice giving women the chance of seeing a doctor of their own sex but, also, reducing the 365 day a year, 24 hour a day responsibility of being a doctor in a village. This pattern does not fit in with responsibilities of a young woman and resulted in the overall change in all GPs' commitment recently. For 20-30 years now, half of medical graduates have been women and, to use their skills, the administrative arrangements of the National Health Service had to change.

Dr. Peter Evans (Cambridge and London) joined in 1979 and Dr. David Sinclair from Dublin replaced Dr. Ellis in 1984. They developed the practice technically in many ways, introducing new methods of diagnosis and treatment; thus needing a larger surgery. The old Lloyd George notes gave way to computers, all-round labour saving, and quicker reaction to demands relating to patients. At the end of the day, one is still left with one doctor with one anxious patient coming through the door; the doctor somehow, at the end, has to make a living out of it, and get satisfaction from it.

Dr. Kenneth Dunton retired in 1994 and was replaced by Dr. Nigel Wade who is the first locally born doctor; Dr. Janet Naylor maintains the feminine side. Titchfield doctors are now totally separated from Park Gate, as the original areas have become separated in many other ways, with so many more people. However the village still remains a very special place.

Kenneth Dunton

NURSE GARDNER

The community of Titchfield had never been short of proficient nurses, but in 1930 the 27 year old Nurse Dorothy Lawson descended on the village, having qualified as a State Registered Nurse, and State Registered Midwife in Bromley, Kent; she subsequently married a local man, Richard Gardner, and became the indomitable Nurse Gardner. Records indicate that, during her time in Titchfield, she delivered over 4000 babies and, it was her claim, she never lost a mother. To describe her as formidable is an understatement, and she steadfastly refused to allow the father to be present at the birth, but she was worshipped by most of the mothers, largely due to her competence, dedication and diligence.

She is particularly remembered by the adult 'lads of the

village', as the person they feared most, if she appeared on the scene when they were up to no good. Eccentricity was, also, one of her traits, and she had a tendency to drive down the middle of the road, in her rush to reach a patient; this was OK during the war, when she had one of the few cars in the village, a pre-war Morris 8, but caused consternation later in her life. She officially retired in 1963, and Wilfred Pickles brought his radio show *'Have A Go'* down to celebrate the event, during which the Carnival Queen of the day presented her with a cheque, from the people of Titchfield, for £146, equivalent to about £3500 today. Also, Gardner Road was named in commemoration of her efforts on behalf of the Parish. In typical fashion, despite being warned not to, she continued to practice her skills when asked, and finally died, aged 79, in 1982, having been blind for the previous 5 years, due to diabetes.

Ken Groves

LEE-ON-THE-SOLENT

Lee-on-the-Solent, once in the Titchfield parish, often referred to as Lee on-Solent, is now a small seaside town about five miles west of Portsmouth. The town is located on the coast of the Solent and forms part of the borough of Gosport. It is primarily a sleepy residential area, with an upsurge of mostly local visitors in summer, but is well known as a former home to the Royal

Naval Air Station HMS Daedalus (previously known as HMS Ariel) and for its booming ice cream trade. In the Middle Ages there were two hamlets called Lee Markes and Lee Brutton.The modern town gained its name from the river Lee, a small stream that flows from Peel Common into the Solent, which was originally used to name hamlets along its length. Two of the hamlets, later called Lower Lee and Middle Lee, were to become Lee-on-the-Solent, while a third hamlet (known as Upper Lee) was to become Peel Common. From the 19th century onward, there were attempts to develop Lee-on-the-Solent as a resort. Early impetus came from Charles Edmund Newton Robinson, who persuaded his father, John Charles Robinson, art curator and collector, to fund the buying of land. Over the period 1884 to 1894 the town was established with the setting out of Marine Parade Pier, a railway connection and a number of impressive red brick villas.

The railway was opened on 12th May 1894 by the Lee on the Solent Company as the seaside terminus of the branch that the LSWR Fareham to Gosport line at Fort Brockhurst. In 1909 the LSWR leased the line and was subsequent

taken over by SR in 1923. But it became a burden, the last train ran on 28th October 1935 and the track was lifted in 1939.

THE TOWER,
LEE-ON-THE-SOLENT.

In 1935 the Lee Tower complex was built on the seafront next to the pier and railway station. It was designed by architects, Yates, Cook and Derbyshire, and comprised a white v-shaped Art Deco building with a 120-foot tower. It housed a cinema, ballroom, restaurant as well as a viewing platform at the tower's peak. The Pier, unrepaired after breaching in aid of coastal defence, was demolished in 1958 and Gosport Council demolished the complex in 1971 and its is now used for the promenade and remembrance gardens.

Lee-on-the Solent has long had an association with flying, with seaplane trials taking place as early as 1917, The Fleet Air Arm there in 1939 and it closed in 1996. Daedalus Base and Airfield (RAF) was the first military branch on this site in 1917. The base was used for a variety of activities, and was a training

Beauties of
LEE-ON-SOLENT

THE PIER

1920s Postcard

Seen on the beach at Lee-on-the-Solent

establishment from the early 1970s until closure. Activities of a historical interest are Seaplanes, the Spitfire equivalent, Hovercraft - military trials as to it suitability in the defence fields, - Search and Rescue (SAR) for the Solent and surrounding sea areas (now undertaken by a commercial contractors (Bristows), and not forgetting the famous Fleet Air Arm Field Gun Crew whose home Daedalus was each year for Field Gun training prior to the Royal Tournament at Earls Court in London, Sadly that event was scrapped in one of the many Defence Reviews undertaken in the 90's.

On 1 April 1920, a School of Naval Co-operation and Aerial Navigation was formed at RAF Calshot to provide seaplane training, with a detachment operating from Lee-on-Solent as the RAF Seaplane Training School. At this time Lee-on-Solent formed one of only four UK naval air stations following the end of the First World War. Its status was assured due to its continuing convenience as a shore base for aircraft of the Royal Navy at nearby Portsmouth. Naval aviation training continued throughout the 1920's under the RAF. Both Calshot and Lee-on-Solent provided training in operating seaplanes, first using the wartime Short Type 184s which was the first ever successful aerial torpedo bomber to sink an enemy ship. Its first kill was a Turkish vessel sunk in the Dardanelles in 1915),.but the air station was gradually acquiring new equipment and from late 1921 was being equipped with the new Fairey IIID. On 1 May 1923, No. 440 (Fleet Reconnaissance) Flight was formed from officers of No. 205 squadron RAF at Lee-on-Solent seaplane base They were equipped with the new Supermarine

Seagull Mk.II biplane amphibian flying boats, and were later to see service in the aircraft carrier HMS Eagle.

On 1 April 1924, naval aviation was formally given the collective title "Fleet Air Arm of the Royal Air Force", and No. 440 Flight joined the School of Naval Co-operation at Lee-on-Solent that year to work up on its new Fairey IIIDs. In the following year it formed a new Fleet Reconnaissance Flight on 15 January 1925 at Lee on Solent for service in the seaplane carrier HMS Vindictive.

The Schneider Trophy was known under various names: Schneider Trophy Schneider Cup, and Flying Flirt. The official name, in French, was "Coupe d'Aviation Maritime Jacques Schneider". The trophy was a work of art costing 25,000 francs. The aero club winning 3 races in 5 years would retain the cup and the winning pilot would receive 75,000 francs. Lee on Solent saw the race in 1929 and 1931. The area was to again see the Schneider trophy competition in July 1995. RAeC Goodyear & Schneider Trophy Air, starting from Bembridge in the Isle of Wight. Each occasion of the race was to be hosted by the previous winning country. The races were to be supervised by the Federation Aeronautique Internationale and the Aero Club in the hosting country. Each club would be permitted to enter up to three competitors with an equal number of alternates. In 1921, the course was increased to 212 nautical miles, with only one authorized take off, after a 2.5 nautical mile water navigation contest. Crowds in excess of 250,000 spectators gathered to watch the Schneider Cup races, proving a keen public interest in this type of competition. In the late 1920s, the great British contender was the Supermarine S6B, which was designed by R.J. Mitchell, the creator of the world famous Supermarine Spitfire of World War II.

The Second World War The Lee on the Solent area was used extensively for the D Day Normandy landings, both training and the eventual departure of ships, landing craft, mulberry pontoons and the men that took part in the invasion. Pier House, which was then the Pier Hotel formerly Hammonds, was used by the Canadian Forces as their Head Quarters. The American Harbour Master, who co-ordinated the landing from these shores - famed as the best in the world at the time - was Tug Wilson. During the Second World War, Gosport Borough played a major role in supplying the Navy and providing the main submarine base. Grange airfield was used to train pilots and HMS Daedalus housed the "Swordfish" torpedo bombers and seaplanes. The airfield was bombed during the Battle of Britain in 1940, killing 14, wounding five and destroying three hangers and 42 aircraft. Mansfield House, which was a hotel in Manor Way, and is now a rest home, opposite the Bun Penny public house, was also bombed. During this raid Flight Lieutenant James Nicholson of 249 Squadron remained at the controls of his blazing Hurricane while continuing his attack on a Messerschmitt 110. He baled out with severe wounds and burns to his hands and face. He became Fighters Command's

only recipient of the Victoria Cross. The Base also played a pivotal role in Operation Overlord. On June 6, 1944. D-Day 435 sorties a one-day record for a single airfield were flown in support of the invasion. By 1944, the whole area was bristling with activity and equipment as it provided a major embarkation centre for D-Day. Stokes Bay, Lee-on-the-Solent, Hardway and Gosport were all used in this massive operation.

Modern Times
The Royal Naval Air Station HMS Daedalus closed in 1996, but remains in use for leisure gliding, and as the base of a HM Coastguard search and rescue helicopter. The site was split up in 2006 with the Maritime & Coastguard Agency (MCA) and South East England Development Agency (SEEDA) largely owning the land. The airfield area was operated by Hampshire Police on behalf of the MCA. Since 2008 there has been a multi-Purpose Driving Test Centre.

In 2003, the community of Lee-on-the-Solent received nationwide attention for probably the first time in its 120-year existence.to abandon the asylum centre plan and the action group celebrated with a rally on the seafront. Whatever the rights and wrongs of the argument, a strong community spirit was evident throughout. Channel 4 produced a fly-on-the-wall Dispatchesdocmentary "Keep them out" in 2004 dealing with both sides of the argument. (Written in 2010).

In early May 2006, 20 unexploded pipe mines were found under HMS Daedalus during runway repairs. 60 feet long, they were left over from 265, packed with a total of 2,400lb of gelignite, planted in World War II to make the airfield unusable in the event of a Nazi invasion. The subsequent removal, thought to be the largest of its kind in peacetime Britain, led to the evacuation of some 900 homes staggered over a 5 week period.

The once bustling shopping centre has good range of independent shops, a couple of corporate shops and a collection of takeaways, charity shops and estate agents. The number of retirement homes has drastically increased, and many people choose to shop at out-of-town outlets, taking some trade away from the High Street. Large new developments in the 1980s and 1990s have swelled the population.

More recently, 1,050 new units have been built at Cherque Farm, area of the town, and further development will take place over the next few years. Elsewhere along Marine Parade, the seafront of this seaside town has lost most of the original villas and hotels to developers. In 2010 several original properties remain boarded up awaiting the fate of the developers' demolition and new buildings constructed. This was not helped by the closure of the Belle Vue Hotel after its planned expansion was halted by local objections, with its subsequent demolition and the building of apartments for the elderly. With commanding views of the Solent and across the Isle of Wight, Lee seafront used to be packed with families and people enjoying the beach nearly all year round. From Browndown right the way along as far as Hill Head in the west, you would be hard pushed to find an isolated spot to sit and enjoy yourself.

Lee no longer has the hotels to attract holiday maker as it once did, today's visitors tend to be day trippers coming from the surrounding area and further afield to enjoy.

Ray Harding

References:

1. Portsmouth - Alan H. Balfour, Peter Hollins, Geoffrey Broadbent, Studio Vista 1970

2. Newsletter- Lee-on-the-Solent Sailing Club, Summer 2003
3. The Book of Gosport - Lesley Burton and Brian Musselwhite 2004
4. Memories of Lee - 2008

LEE SCHOOL

The Lee-on-the-Solent Temporary County School, know as the "Tin School" opened on September 18th 1905, Head, Grace A Malcomber. Classes, divided by a red curtain,

were mixed and included infants; total number of pupils 50. Drills were substituted for singing on very cold mornings in January 1906, and in May 1905 special lessons on the Empire "Flag of England" recited and National Anthem sung to encourage patriotism. Flu closed the school in January 1907 for two weeks. On the 14th August 1908 the Temporary School closed and was demolished and the new School opened on the 28th September 1908. Number of pupils was 101, aged from 3 years upwards. There was

no proper playground, so the pupils just ran around outside until the bell rang.. The school has served generations of pupils and celebrated its 100th birthday on the 28 September 2008, when pupils took photographs around Lee that are now on a permanent display inside the School.   **Maureen Williams**

HOLLY HILL WOODLAND PARK

Holly Hill Woodland Park has been recognised as an outstanding woodland park and originated as the water garden of Sarisbury Court. The picture is a view of the lower lake.

When the original mansion was built the valley was bisected by a stream which rises just beyond Sarisbury Green. The West slope of the valley was relatively gentle and used as grass meadow, but the Eastern slope was steeper and predominantly unstable clay prone to slumping and only suitable for coppice woodland.

The Tithe Map of 1838 records the 'Long Meadow' and 'Wood Blow Garden' beside the walled garden to of Holly Hill House. These are now overgrown and contain large trees. A small triangular 'duck' pond is shown at the Southern end of the existing system in the estate maps of 1867, and this is also shown on the first Ordnance Survey carried out in 1866, though not published until 1881.

Edward Light records the landscape gardeners digging the lake system shortly after Quentin Hogg purchased the estate in 1879. This equates to a construction date of approximately 1801, a date confirmed by tree ring data for yew trees contemporary with digging of the lakes. The Title Deeds for the estate record an essentially linear lake system with an inlet at the lower end giving access to a boathouse. A carriageway sweeps down from the house, now renamed

Sarisbury Court, to cross the lakes in a central iron bridge and exit via a lodge on Barnes Lane. This lodge remains as 61 Barnes Lane. When the estate was broken up in 1898 the lakes, together with Cawtes Copse, was bought by Montague Henry Foster, a property developer who reworked the eastern edge of the lakes into their present 'Romantic Wilderness' form, and created islands. He also roofed the grotto to form a mysterious cave structure and planted the Chestnut Avenue.

Foster sold the estate to George Winn in 1898 who began building a new Holly Hill House beside Barnes Lane in 1905. The sand pit, first shown in 1896, was the location of three large glasshouses, and extensive gardens were laid out around the house. The glasshouses, in a poor condition, were demolished in the 1920's and the area turned into a sunken garden. The photograph is one of Katherine Winn's pictures of the sunken garden taken in the 1920's. The sunken garden has recently been restored in a less labour-intensive form. It is probable that there was replanting of the lake land area after Winn built his house, and the flight of ponds which descend the eastern

183

slope date from this period. A vista, probably grassed, ran down from the house to the lakes and is shown on the maps of 1910. Winn also acquired a strip of agricultural land to the east of Cawtes Copse, which enabled him to extend a carriageway along the top of the slope and, via an embankment, out to a landing stage on the Hamble sea wall. This remained an access until broken down when Bunny Meadow was flooded in about 1943. A second lodge was built to control the approach to the new house. This remains as Holly Hill Lodge, between the cemetery and Barnes Lane.

The death of George Winn resulted in the estate being sold to William Rilley of Port Hamble Ltd on the 3rd of December 1947. Donald Session of Port Hamble Ltd retained a portion, and sold the remainder to Fareham Urban District Council for £6,500 on the 14th of April 1954. They created the cemetery and Winnards Park estate and developed the lakeland site into the present Holly Hill Woodland Park.

In 1975 Fareham Borough Council entered into a contract with Community Industry to refurbish the neglected site. Community Industry was a government initiative to train unemployed school leavers and, with The National Association of Boys Clubs, supplied the labour and paid the wages of the staff and workers who refurbish the park. Unemployed school leavers were used to clear the lakes and create the present paths, and their work was completed by 1985. A ranger service was developed in 2002, who with the 'Friends of Holly Hill' maintain the present site. This involves removing invasive laurel, building fences, repairing paths and generally keeping the park in reasonable order.

During a normal year about twelve trees fall naturally. Those that block paths or are dangerous are removed but those which fall in the less accessible areas are left to decay and provide sites for invertebrates and thus feeding sites for other wild life. Most of the fallen trees are Birches which are short lived and replaced naturally, but, on average, a large Oak or Beech falls every couple of years. Since these are often over 150 years old they are less readily replaced. There are also a number of less common trees, planted when the site was open park land. Many of these are over 150 years old and approaching the end of their life, and a programme of replacement has been carried out, planting 10 year old trees to ensure the park retains its quality. These have been predominately planted to maintain variety and ensure good autumn colour, using trees such as Liquid Amber, Red Oaks, Pin Oaks and some conifers.

David Redwood

TITCHFIELD HAVEN NATIONAL NATURE RESERVE

Over the last fifty years there has been a noticeable expansion in urban and industrial development in Hampshire, which has put mounting pressure on our countryside. To counter this pressure a policy of protecting Hampshire's coast through land acquisition was adopted by the County Council in 1972 resulting in the purchase of Titchfield Haven and subsequent areas of threatened habitats along the coast. This ownership of a number of nature reserves, some of which are of outstanding ornithological importance, has guaranteed protection to a wide variety of habitats and their associated wildlife.

Titchfield Haven, lying to the south of the village of Titchfield, was formerly the estuary of the River Meon which up until the early 17th Century allowed craft to serve the port of Titchfield. The then owner of the land, the Third Earl of Southampton, was responsible for the building of a bund across the mouth of the estuary that was completed in 1611. The resulting reclaimed land was later drained to enable cattle grazing and hay cutting. The transformation of such a large area of tidal saltmarsh to freshwater marshland would have brought about considerable changes in the birdlife. Wildfowling would have become a regular pastime whilst surface feeding duck are attracted to the marshes. In the early 1820s much of the area known as Titchfield Estate was owned by the Delme' Family, and was familiar to the celebrated wildfowler Colonel Peter Hawker. The hunting of wildfowl continued throughout the 19th Century and on into the first part of the 20th Century, finally ceasing in 1945. From 1929 until 1972, much of Titchfield Haven was owned and maintained by the late Colonel Alston and his family, primarily as private grazing land. As the only access at this time was permitted to grazing tenants, fishermen and to birdwatchers under the guidance of local amateur ornithologists, the site was able to function as a private sanctuary for a host of wetland birds. Official recognition of the Haven as an important wetland came in 1959 when the then Nature Conservancy Council declared much of the area as a Site of Special Scientific Interest (SSSI).

Following the purchase of Titchfield Haven from the Alston family in 1972, a Naturalist Warden was appointed, and then four years of preparatory work involved the building of observation hides and connecting walkways, as well

as landscaping and the installation of water control measures. Finally the site was opened to the visiting public in October 1976. At about this time the Haven was declared a Local Nature Reserve (LNR) under section 19/21 of the National Parks and Access to the Countryside Act 1949. The protection this declaration gave Titchfield Haven was just the beginning of the conservation story. Successful management led to the site achieving greater recognition in 1995 when declared a National Nature Reserve (NNR), by which time further land purchases by the County Council had increased the reserve to over 300 acres. The development of Haven House as the nature reserve's Visitor Centre was made possible in 1998 following a successful bid for Heritage Lottery funding. The Centre now houses staff offices, interpretation displays, a shop, tea-room and a functions room.

Today Titchfield Haven is an important sanctuary for a number of nationally rare breeding and migratory birds, including Avocets, Cetti's Warblers and Bearded Reedlings. Each year over one hundred and seventy species of birds can be expected to be recorded with over sixty remaining to breed. Management of four miles of the coast to the west of Titchfield Haven by Countryside Service staff, including the 1200 acre Chilling Farm Estate, and the 560 acres of the Hook with Warsash nature reserve at the mouth of the Hamble River, offers further interest and enjoyment to birdwatchers and walkers, and acts as a buffer to urban development.

Barry Duffin

WHITE CANONS IN TITCHFIELD, JULY 2011

Edward Roberts in his article 'Dating Titchfield's Buildings' (above) has shown that No. 1 Place House Cottage, in the background to our photograph, was first built in the fifteenth century as the monastic grammar school of Titchfield Abbey, which had been founded by Praemonstratensian Canons in 1232. Dressed in white habits, they would have been in many parts of Titchfield during the three hundred years of the abbey's existence. In particular, they would have been the schoolmasters at the school.

I live in the former Grammar School, now Place House Cottage, and have been delighted in helping to preserve this important building for future generations. In early July 2011, we were busy undertaking the last of our current refurbishments, when we heard a voice enquiring after the keys to Place House.

fr. Julien   fr. Maximillien   fr. Dominique-Marie   fr. Laurent

Imagine my surprise on looking out and seeing four men in white robes standing in our garden - Praemonstratensian Canons. Had I been transported back 500 years, or was I suffering from hallucinations? No, they were indeed White Canons, from the Abbey of Mondaye in Normandy, here to view the ruins of the Abbey their Order had built and occupied for 300 years. Sadly, the Abbey was temporarily closed, but they were given a short lecture on local history, and shown views of the Abbey from around the site.

Their timetable was very tight, but before they left in their Citroen they agreed to be photographed with the Old Grammar School in the background. The Canon in charge was fr. Dominique Marie who was the Master to the young Canons, fr. Julien, fr. Maximilian and fr. Laurent. They are intending to come back again to look round the Abbey, the Grammar School and the village of which they were once landlords.

White Canons have visited the Abbey from time to time since 1537, but this was the first time any of them had seen the grammar school at which their predecessors had taught. We were delighted that this will not be the last.

Ken Groves

1300 YEARS OF AN ANCIENT PARISH

St. Peter's, the church of the ancient parish, was founded in the years just before and after 700 AD. The ancient parish, which has been the subject of this volume, grew around the church for more than a millennium, becoming a basic administrative unit as well as a centre of worship. This ancient parish saw the Norman Conquest, the arrival of a monastic community, the dissolution of the monasteries, the Armada, the Civil War, the battle of Waterloo, and many changes to the natural environment.

During the 19th century, the administrative functions of the ancient parish withered away: new ecclesiastical parishes and new civil parishes were created. In the 20th century most of the ancient parish became part of the borough of Fareham. But Titchfield remains an ecclesiastical parish, and worship continues at the ancient church as it has for 300 years.

Rev Susan Allman 2011

George Watts

VICARS OF TICHFIELD

1302 JOHN de NIWETONE		1919 GEORGE S MORLEY
c1316 WALTER de TICHFEND	1563 JOHN CARDEN	1936 FRANK E SPURWAY
c1323 HENRY de SPERSHOLT	1572 ROBERT GARNET	1947 NORMAN A J MILLER
1332 PETER de WYNTON	1587 WILLIAM PARKER	1973 THOMAS W W PEMBERTON
1348 WILLIAM de WOLLOP	1602 FRANCIS BRADSELL	1992 JAMES A MITCHELL-INNES
1349 THOMAS de AMBRESBURY	1610 NICHOLAS MUNON	1998 BILL DAY
1361 WALTER OXNEFORDE	1616 HENRY TILLEY	
1361 WILLIAM de CLAVERLI	1623 TIMOTHY BLEIR	
1369 GILBERT de LOVENTE	1640 JAMES LAMB (EJECTED)	
1370 RICHARD de TICHFFELD	1642 URIAH OAKES (EJECTED)	
1395 JOHN ESTFELD	1670 WALTER GARRETT	
1413 WILLIAM CORBET	1683 ALEXANDER BRUCE	
1435 EDWARD TANNER	1729 MICHAEL WHITE	
1462 WILLIAM HAMPTON	1746 GILBERT JACKSON	
1465 JOHN PAPPEWORTH	1791 ALEXANDER RADCLIFFE	
1485 WILLIAM LAMBE	1826 WILLIAM THRESHER	
1522 THOMAS GODFREY	1852 WALTER M COSSER	
1539 MARTIN TYNDALL	1887 REGINALD A R WHITE	
1558 JOHN PERYE	1907 CHARLES E MATTHEWS	

Rev Jane Richasrds 2010

St Peter's Church Palm Sunday Procession

The Titchfield History Society would like to thank the Hampshire Record Office, the Local Libraries and the many members of the public who have given generous help and advice to our contributors.

This is the third of our selections of incidents and issues from the long history of the ancient parish,. Many more topics are still to be explored, We commend this task to the next generation.

Errata
P6, P107: for "Charles II" read "Charles I";
P78, P80: for "(Fig 1)" read "(P70, Fig 2)"

George Watts

Place House Chimneys

FURTHER READING

The publications of the Titchfield History Society 1. Titchfield: A History, 1982; 2. Titchfield: A Place in History, 1989; 3. Titchfield Parish Register 1589-1634, 1998; 4. Titchfield Parish Register 1634-1678, 2006; 5. Titchfield at the Start of the Third Millenium, 2000; which contains an extensive bibliography of published material on Titchfield and The Hearth Tax Return for the Hundred of Titchfield, 1985.

6. Eyewitness Account, 2007, is published jointly by the Titchfield Wordwrights and Titchfield History Society. Two other local publications are Four Centuries of the Earl of Southampton Trust, Earl of Southampton Trust, 1997; and The Titchfield Village Trust, by Frank Waddell, 1993. Two recent books on the history of the area are The River Hamble: A History, by David Chun, 2009, and Villages of the Meon Valley, by Peter Watkins, 2010.

Timber-framed houses in the parish are described in Hampshire Houses 1250-1 700, by Edward Roberts, 2003. The Stubbington History Society and the Warsash History Society publish regularly on local topics. As most of the ancient parish is now in Fareham Borough the twice-yearly Fareham: Past and Present, ed. Pam Wenden, frequently includes Titchfield topics; as do the publications of the Hampshire Field Club and Archaeological Society, which include the annual Hampshire Studies and its twice-yearly Newsletter.

Further information about publications can be found on the Titchfield History Society website: http://www.communigate.co.uk/hants/ths

Index

A

Abbots, list	22
Anne, Queen	29

B

Barlow, Andrew	
Victoria Brewery, Southampton	166
Beer Houses and Inns	160
Bourmaster, Admiral	130
Burrell, John	105
Bypass A27	150

C

Chamberlain, Sir Austen	
British Secretary of State	143
Chilcott, Sir Warden	141
Chilling	55
Coach and Horses	117
Cooper, Allan	
Warash	156
Crofton Church	
Holy Rood	15

D

Delmé, Sir Henry, Peter	162
Doctors in Titchfield	168
Draper, Chris	
Archeologist	
Hill Head	8
Dudley, Henry	55
Duffin, Barry	188

F

Fielder, John	
Titchfield Brewer	166

G

Gardner, Nurse	174

H

Hack, Brian	9
Henrietta Queen	
Charles II King	107
Holly Hill	182
Hook at Hamble mouth	27
Hornby	
Gov. Bombay	
Hook House, Titchfield	137
Hurdens of Titchfield	157

I

Iron Age site	
Segensworth fish ponds	12
Ives Family	127

L

Leach, Pip	35
Lee School	181
Lee Tower	176
Lee-on-the-Solent Airfield	176
Lewthwaite, John. C,	81
Lychgate Green,	
Crofton	15

M

Mapull, William	
Mayor of Southampton	28
Margaret of Anjou	
Wife of Henry V	48
Mary, Queen	99
Meon	
New River	67
Mills, Julia R,	115
Missing, Thomas	112

N

Nature Conservancy	185

P

Pepys, Samuel
Flag Officer listings 132
Plantagenet, Arthur 49
Popely, Patsy
Life member Titchfield Bonfire Boys 5
Postscript 192
Premonstratensian Abbey 22
Prestidge, Colin
Crofton Church 21

R

Redwood, David
Sarisbury 149
Richard II 36
Richard II, Queen Anne
Hand baggage cart 29
Roberts, Edward 45

S

Sarisbury Court 146
Saxton, Christopher
map maker 59
Schneider Trophy
Air Race 178
Sea Lock
67, 81, 82
Segensworth Iron Age Site 12
St. Peter, parish church ofbooklet
available in church 86

T

Timberlake, Henry
merchant adventurer 103

Titchfield Beacon
part of country signalling sys. 46
Titchfield Haven 121
Titchfield History Society
browse for THS 5
Titchfield Parish Reghister
death of Timberlake 1625 106
Titchfield Parish Register
the Missings 113

U

University of Southampton
Hack Collection
Brian Hack 9

V

Vernon, Elizabth
Wife of Henry Wriothesley 101

W

Wartime in Sarisbury Green 155

Williams, Maureen
Lee School 181
Woolgar, C.M. 65

Gargoyle from Titchfield Abbey

The End

Printed by Sarsen Press Printers
22 Hyde Street, Winchester